Forest School Wild Play

Forest School Wild Play

Outdoor Fun with Nature's Elements
Earth, Air, Fire & Water

Jane Worroll - *Illustrated by* Peter Houghton

WATKINS

Sharing Wisdom Since
1893

Forest School Wild Play
Jane Worroll - Illustrated by Peter Houghton

First published in the UK and USA in 2021 by
Watkins, an imprint of Watkins Media Limited
Unit 11, Shepperton House, 83–93 Shepperton Road
London N1 3DF

enquiries@watkinspublishing.com

Commissioning Editor: Fiona Robertson
Editorial Assistant: Brittany Willis
Head of Design: Glen Wilkins
Art Director: Karen Smith
Production: Uzma Taj
Commissioned artwork: Peter Houghton

A CIP record for this book is available
from the British Library

ISBN: 978-1-78678-420-9 (Paperback)
ISBN: 978-1-78678-582-4 (eBook)

10 9 8 7 6 5 4 3 2 1

Typeset in Archer
Printed in Slovenia

www.watkinspublishing.com

PUBLISHER'S NOTE:
Some activities in this book, for example
those involving fire or cutting tools, may be
dangerous if instructions are not followed
precisely. Always follow manufacturers'
instructions when using tools. Wild foods
such as berries can be poisonous, so eat only
what you can identify as safe. Adults need to
assess each child's capabilities and supervise
any potentially dangerous activity at all times.
Watkins Media Limited, or any other persons
who have been involved in working on this
publication, cannot accept responsibility for
any injury, illness or damages that result from
participating in the activities in this book.

CONTENTS

Introduction

It was once believed that all creation, including ourselves, was formed from the four elements: earth, air, fire and water. For everyone at Forest School, these four elements are tangibly all around us in the earth underfoot, the patter of rain on a shelter, the warmth of campfire flames and the wind on our faces. In our outdoor activities we can connect with the elements by mixing natural dyes in water (page 138), gathering wood for a Dakota fire pit (page 99), moulding clay dug from the earth (page 22) and blowing air through handmade wooden whistles (page 71).

The four elements have been embedded in the human psyche for thousands of years and became deeply rooted in many cultures around the world, including those of ancient Greece, India and Tibet. The elements have formed the basis of ancient calendars, medicine, astrology and myths, and lie at the foundations of many spiritual traditions. Modern science, of course, does not support the view that these classical elements are the material basis of the physical world. Science did, however, grow in its understanding from this fundamental four.

The elements do not exist in isolation, but are influenced by and connected to one another and ourselves. We have come to realize globally how our actions can damage the earth, the oceans and the air. Equally, we understand how we can harness the power of the sun and wind to generate cleaner energy – and how we can all contribute to maintaining a healthy planet for all species to share and benefit from.

With so much negative news around about the result of our human impact on the planet, during our Forest School sessions, we feel it is truly empowering and beneficial to share knowledge and skills with children about how they can make a positive difference to this world through even the smallest of actions. We aim to share some of these ideas throughout this book, which has a core message of sustainability and focuses on the amazing web of life.

In each chapter, activities link to one of the four elements and there is a special focus on storytelling and imagination, helping kids to form an emotional and moral connection to the natural world and build a sense of belonging and community. We believe it's through developing a connection, an awareness and an understanding of our common bond to the natural world that our actions can become more harmonious and empathetic for all creatures. And what better way to bond with the natural world than to spend amazing fun days immersed within it, as we do at Forest School.

WHY NATURE?

If you're an adult, you can probably remember spending many hours each week playing outdoors as a child, heading off first thing after breakfast and not coming back home until tea time. There wouldn't be a grown-up in sight while you explored woodlands, building sites and parks, playing games with friends in the street, climbing trees, testing boundaries and taking risks all for the sheer fun of it.

Many of us now live in societies where, compared to those of previous generations, people spend more and more time indoors, and where parents unfortunately feel deterred from allowing their children to play outside. This is, in part, due to the ever-increasing loss of green space, particularly in urban environments. There is also a greater fear of strangers, traffic and accidents, and a lack of time due to our busy, overscheduled lives – along with ubiquitous technology designed to constantly pull our attention, especially that of children.

While technology has its valid place, it's the imbalance of its use in many of our children's lives that is the issue. One study found that children today spend twice as long looking at screens than playing outside, and more than half of this time for some will be solitary screen-based activities without their family or friends, often continuing late into the night. Not only has this sort of sedentary lifestyle contributed to the obesity epidemic for adults and children in the developed world, but many scientists believe our brains are simply not designed for this complex 24/7 world, with its constant bombardment of information. There has been, sadly, a stark rise in children and teenagers suffering from mental health disorders. Whilst more research is needed, negative social media use and lack of sleep have been cited as contributing factors, alongside another key change: the increasing amount of time we spend indoors.

As most of us will know, research shows that physical activity has a positive effect in keeping us healthy. If this physical activity takes place outside in a natural setting, there are further benefits: sunlight and soil microorganisms can boost the body's levels of serotonin, a chemical linked to feelings of wellbeing, while vitamin D, essential for bone and muscle health, is also provided by the sun's rays. More recently, however, studies have concluded that there's something about simply being in nature that has a beneficial effect on reducing stress and mental fatigue, and increasing our attention capacity, critical thinking and resilience. It also promotes self-motivation and the ability to connect with other people and nature itself, leading to improved feelings of wellbeing, creativity and environmental stewardship. These are all skills that are vitally important for kids to thrive in the 21st century, and indeed are key to sustaining a healthy future for us all on this magnificent planet, our home.

Forest School always takes place in a natural setting and as such has the potential to provide participants with an opportunity to spend time in nature with all the resulting benefits – particularly for those who may often feel estranged from the natural world.

WHAT IS FOREST SCHOOL?

Forest School is defined by the Forest School Association as "an inspirational process that offers all learners regular opportunities to achieve and develop confidence and self-esteem through hands-on learning experiences in a woodland or natural environment with trees". Forest School sessions are now offered in a huge range of settings – from city parks, private land and rural forests to beaches and indeed jungles. These sessions are organized by many different providers, including mainstream schools, specialist outdoor kindergartens, private businesses running term-time, holiday and after-school clubs, and agencies countering addiction, health issues and social exclusion. However, they all have this in common: they take place in a natural environment where a qualified leader aims to provide a nurturing space that supports every learners' wellbeing.

Through close observation of each individual child's learning process and the innate way that child interacts with the world and mentoring, a Forest School leader can provide opportunities for different experiences that can help each child to learn more effectively. These experiences can also foster traits such as resilience, independence, confidence and emotional intelligence that will support the learner throughout their lives. Within this framework the participants are given ownership over their journey to follow their interests and cultivate their learning at their own pace. To fully embed learning and develop a sense of community and a greater sense of connection with nature, Forest School sessions have a high adult-to-child (or participant) ratio and take place with the same group on a regular, long-term basis.

We use a variety of locations for our own Forest School sessions and repeated visits make each of these sites familiar to our groups. This helps children feel a sense of belonging and gain confidence by allowing them to get to know each other and the boundaries (both physical and behavioural), as well as where their basic needs can be met – where they will eat and where they can shelter (in dens or under tarps, for example), and the location of the toilets and hand-washing facilities. From this basis, interests can be freely followed and deeper learning of practised skills explored and mastered. Unlike tightly regulated and confined school classrooms, the open surroundings of Forest School sites allow children greater personal control over social interactions, as there is freedom for all to move around and consciously choose the space they occupy, which helps relationships build in a more relaxed atmosphere. The opportunity and freedom to make their own independent choices within play also gives children the space to be themselves.

In developing a sense of community, the leader will facilitate effective communication, collaboration, empathy and teamwork. Forest School is based on the process of learning rather than on the content of the sessions, encouraging a spontaneous engagement with nature and venturing into the world of the unplanned with all its unlimited and unexpected discoveries. This combination of factors and of actual experiences in nature are key to creating a collaborative community, building self-esteem and developing learning that lasts over time, as well as encouraging a greater sense of connection to nature and an understanding of a shared sustainable future – all of which make Forest School so effective.

THE FOREST SCHOOL SESSION

In Forest School, each session has a clear beginning and ending. Before we start, to help every child (especially anyone new) feel confident and at ease, the boundaries of the play area and the rules regarding safety and care for each other and the environment are established. We also point out where the toilets are, where food will be kept and where we can wash our hands and shelter.

In groups, it can be helpful to sit in a circle during this opening time, taking it in turns to share thoughts and feelings. This can help to gauge the children's mood and energy levels, and be used as an indication to look at or offer an activity that may be appropriate for children seeking particular guidance. You can either ask them directly how they feel (especially if you are looking after young children, just one child or a relatively small group) or, with larger numbers (and especially older children), you could suggest they rate their mood on a scale of one to ten. This often encourages children to share their feelings.

The same technique can be used at the end of the session, when we like to round off the day by inviting the children to share how they now feel and provide an opportunity for them to reflect on their experiences. As well as helping the children to process the day, this encourages them to play an active role in their own learning. And these discussions are a fantastic way to gain insight into what worked and what could be adjusted about each activity, providing a valuable guide for future sessions. Remember, however, that these are only invitations to share and some children may be too shy at first.

NATURE'S ELEMENTS AND FOREST SCHOOL

In this book, we offer a wide range of Forest School activities to tie in with the natural elements of earth, air, fire and water. In choosing these activities, we have been inspired by the children that we meet and what nature offers, such as digging in the earth to find clay and letting creativity run loose to mould all manner of things; listening to the low drone of a bullroarer as it's whirled through the air; building a Dakota fire pit to gather around for storytelling and to drink birch twig tea; or constructing wonderful watertight dens.

We have also supplied a story for each element to inspire a love for the ancient art of oral storytelling and to share knowledge, laugh and journey together, and to build a sense of community and an emotional connection to the natural world. Two of the stories are Jane's retellings of old myths and two are Jane's own creation. We have found that, despite these modern times with high-tech games and instant access to media, children love to listen to spoken stories – often joining in with actions, adding to them and making them their own. We have had many amazing story sessions where the atmosphere becomes focused and calm, our imaginations travelling together through the story as it unfolds – and not forgetting many hilarious moments, especially with impromptu mime.

GUIDING A SESSION

It's important to point out that this book is not a replacement for the full experience of going to Forest School (if your child has not done this already, please consider trying it out!), but it does offer a taster of some of the wonderful Forest School activities we use. We've written it for anyone who wants to spend more time outdoors with the children in their care, whether you are a parent, guardian, teacher or youth worker; we also hope it will be a handy resource for Forest School leaders. Whoever you are, the aim is to emulate a Forest School leader by being fully present, enthusiastic, encouraging, inspiring and observant. To create a safe space whereby children have the opportunity to engage with their peers, have the freedom to be themselves within play, assess risks and be creative with what nature offers. Be there to help out with an activity and demonstrate new skills when needed, but allow the learning to be led by the child.

A Forest School leader will also reflect on how each session went for every child individually and encourage children to reflect on their own experiences, too. This information is used to shape future sessions with the aim of providing opportunities for each child to grow and develop as a whole – physically, mentally, emotionally, spiritually and socially. Learning outcomes (which are not an exhaustive list) are provided within this book for each activity and may be useful for planning.

Each elemental chapter offers a range of different activities – some high energy and some requiring more focused participation. The more familiar you become with the activities, the easier it will be to switch between them as needed. For example, you may have a group where not all the children know each other. It is a warm day and the energy levels are high, so a team game, such as the Screaming Game (see page 56) or Feed the Fire (see page 126), would be a fantastic ice breaker and way to start. Once some of that initial energy has been released, the children's attention can then be turned to crafts, such as carving a log cup (see page 164) or playing with clay (see page 22).

A BRIEF GUIDE
Before you try an activity, bear the following points in mind:

→ These activities are suitable for a wide age range (from pre-school children up to teens and even beyond), with a different level of adult guidance needed for different age groups. Assess the individual capabilities of each child before you start and adjust accordingly.

→ For each activity we've suggested a kit list, but we also recommend you bring a first-aid kit, a bag for litter and hand-cleaning supplies if they're not available nearby.

→ If an activity requires more than one child to take part, the ideal number is always stated in the activity.

→ Activities can take place in all weathers (except high winds in woods), so make sure children have suitable clothes for the weather – waterproof clothing and suitable boots can make the difference between a fun day out and a miserable one!

→ Make sure there are enough adults present to allow children to engage in achievable, challenging activities in a safe space.

→ Demonstrate any tricky techniques at the start of each activity, then let the children attempt each step, offering positive encouragement, and only assisting if required.

→ Let kids work things out for themselves if they want to. We've designed the step-by-step instructions and diagrams to be as simple and easily grasped as possible.

Play Safe

Any activity that involves foraging for wild food,
tool use or fire does contain an element of risk,
but by referring back to the guidelines below as you
work through this book and implementing the basic
safety procedures outlined, you will be more than
ably equipped to avoid any potential mishaps.
Above all, the activities in this book are designed
to be interactive, educational, inspirational – and fun.

TOOL USE

Whether an adult is using tools alone or children are handling them
under adult supervision, follow manufacturers' guidelines and the
safety procedures outlined below.

The age at which children are able to use tools under adult
supervision varies, so assess each child individually. If you are
confident that the child is capable, allow tool use. However, close
adult supervision is still required. As a general rule (apart from
knife work when one-on-one is advisable), have one adult watching
a maximum of four capable older kids and a higher adult-to-child
ratio with younger ones for safety.

For extra protection when using tools, a gardening glove can be worn
on helper (non-working) hands (i.e. the hand stabilizing the item or
both hands of children whose role is simply to hold the item), but not
on the working hand (the hand holding the tool) as this can lessen

the grip. Stress that all tools must go back to an adult when they're no longer in use, at which point they should be stored out of the way with all security catches on.

Before embarking on using any tool, demonstrate its use in full to every member of your group following the guide below:

→ Tell everyone the name of the tool that they will be using and what it is used for.
→ Show everyone the cover (if it has one), how to take it off and put it on or how to open and close it.
→ Show them the handle and the cutting edge of the tool.
→ Demonstrate how each tool works.
→ Show how best to position their hands in order to use it safely and cleanly, and how to carry it safely: covered or closed at your side, with the blade pointing toward the floor, and no running!
→ Explain about the safe working zone: this is a circle the diameter of the tool and the user's outstretched arms. If anyone (apart from your partner) enters this circle, the tool user should stop until the zone is empty again.

How to Use a Sheath Knife

For extra safety, it's worth going over the instructions for a sheath knife in detail. Show the knife to everyone, pointing out the blade, cover and handle. Show how, by placing one gloved hand at the tip end of the blade, you are able to pull the cover off and then clip it back on. Once off again, point to the blade's cutting edge. Explain that it is a great tool for carving wood. If possible, sit off the ground, on a stump for example, and with a gloved hand put the wood you are carving to one side of your body. With the knife in the other ungloved hand, carve the wood away from your body. Point out that you always carve away from your body and have no limbs underneath or hands in front of the blade. If sitting cross-legged on the floor, either carve to one side of your body or place elbows on knees and carve away from your body – again, making sure there are no limbs underneath or in front of the blade. (Use this technique with potato peelers as good practice for knife work.)

FORAGING

Being able to positively identify edible wild foods is vital as many plants are poisonous. Always take a field guide with you or use your smartphone to access pictures and information on edible plants, and choose to forage wild foods that can be easily identified. Always check if any of your group have any allergies before foraging for wild food, particularly nuts. Make sure to pick wild food away from pollution sources such as roads, dog-walking spots and sprayed farm margins.

CONSERVATION

We share this planet with many species who rely on the natural larder as their only source of food. With this in mind, think sustainably, spread your foraging over as large an area as possible, and never over-harvest or uproot any plant. Follow local regulations about what you can and cannot pick and, if necessary, check with the landowner first.

FIRE SAFETY

The following fire safety rules are applicable to all types of Forest School fire:

→ Before lighting a fire, check the ground conditions: never light a fire on peaty soil (it is flammable), and remember that porous rocks can also explode. Push any flammable material away from the fire area, and dowse this area with water in very dry weather. Check for and remove any trip hazards.

→ Keep the fire small and usable.

→ Do not burn woods that give off toxic fumes such as elder or painted timbers. (If you are unsure, do a search online before building your fire.)

→ Before using the fire, tie back all long hair and secure any dangling jewellery and clothing.

→ An adult must supervise lit fires at all times.

→ To contain the fire site and mark out the fire boundary that should not be crossed, place a 1m (3ft) square frame of logs/branches around the fire site.

→ No running, pushing or games should occur around the fire site.

FIRE SAFETY KIT

Always have the following items close by when working with fire:

- an open container of water
- a fire blanket (for first aid and to put out fire)
- welding gloves (or equivalent fire-resistant material for handling hot items)
- first-aid box

→ Only those cooking or sitting should be around the fire site. To limit accidents and increase balance and stability, have anyone cooking on or tending the fire kneel on one knee.

→ Extinguish the fire properly before leaving. Let it die down and then spread the ashes out and douse with water until cool to touch. For temporary fire sites, either spread the cold ash around, bury it or take it off site so that you leave no trace.

EARTH

Earth, soil, dirt, mud ... the words used to describe this element don't tend to conjure up glorious images. It can be overlooked or even seen as a nuisance when we have to sweep it up and scrape it off our shoes. But this wonderful material is where our food is grown and where our water is stored. It is home to billions of organisms, not least the earthworms, fungi and bacteria that recycle nutrients, and provides the mycelium that connect plants, like nature's internet, allowing them to communicate with each other and providing a host of benefits to us humans too. All of which is pretty amazing for a clump of mud!

At Forest School, we decorate trees with mud faces, giving the forest a whole new character. We dig deep into its darkness to find treasures such as smooth stones ideal for painting and clay for moulding. We cast animal prints left in the wet soil and we whoosh down exhilarating slippery mud slides. The hours pass by unnoticed while we play and experiment with gooey mud and all sorts of creativity and fun are unleashed. If that still isn't enough reason to love earth, research has shown that playing with soil is good for our health.

Our planet is called Earth, a word meaning ground, the place from which all life springs. So what's not to love about earth? This chapter provides some of our favourite earth activities, so go on – get muddy!

CLAY PLAY

Clay has such a wonderful texture. When wet, it feels slightly sticky and dense. Its surface becomes shiny when rubbed, yet when pinched between fingers it feels smooth. It can be squeezed, stretched and moulded into many shapes. By making a 3D model of an object with clay, you get a chance to connect more deeply with it, what it looks like and what the real thing may feel like. If it doesn't work out, it's not a problem: just squidge it back down into a ball and start again. Then – like magic – clay becomes firm to the touch when it dries, and when it's fired in a kiln, it changes into pottery. It can be used to make many things, such as bowls, bricks, tiles and even musical instruments such as clay flutes.

This wonderful activity unleashes the imagination and clears away any doubts about getting our hands muddy. Making clay requires focus, the need to follow instructions and patience – all while learning about the properties of soil, connecting us more deeply to nature. Working with clay is one of our favourite Forest School activities, especially when it comes to sharing and admiring all the marvellous creations afterwards. What will you make?

TRY THIS!
If anyone is nervous about getting muddy hands, we have found it helps if adults get fully involved, so roll up your sleeves and dig in.

LOCATION	Any natural area with mud

AGE GROUP	2 years +

LEARNING ABOUT ...	⩔ Sensory experiences ⩔ physics ⩔ soil science ⩔ creativity ⩔ focus ⩔ patience ⩔ independence ⩔ nature connections ⩔ freedom ⩔ tool use ⩔ fine and gross motor skills ⩔ communication

KIT	⇀ Spade to share, or one spade each ⇀ Water (*if digging for clay, enough to dampen the clay if it's a hot, dry day; if making clay, enough to cover half a bucketful of soil and a little extra for sieving and cleaning*) ⇀ Tupperware or similar container ⇀ Clothes that can get muddy	If making clay from soil (can *take at least a day*): ⇀ Two buckets ⇀ Large stick for mixing mud ⇀ Fine-mesh sieve ⇀ Empty clear glass/ plastic container such as a 5l (1 gallon) water bottle or wide neck jar ⇀ Old cotton t-shirt, pillow case or other tightly woven material large enough to cover your buckets ⇀ String

OPTIONAL	⇀ Blanket or floor tarp to sit on, funnel, trowel if no spade is available

Get ready

Although gardeners would disagree, we are lucky that our Forest School sites in London sit on top of a lot of clay soil, which is made visible by water logging in wet weather and cracking in hot, dry weather. When the soil is wet, the suction created is so great it can pull your shoe clean off – we have seen many boots get stuck this way! If the soil in your local area is also clay rich, go out and find a suitable spot to set up your clay-digging station. Choose a section of bare earth or somewhere that is only covered in grass or other common species.

If your local area is not heavy with clay, you can make your own clay from soil. It is useful to have a water source nearby as you will need it for covering the soil and sieving it. Whether you are digging for clay or making it from soil, make sure you have the landowner's permission to dig, if necessary. To make sure you do not harm any creatures living in the soil, always check through it and remove them if necessary, then return them to the location where the soil came from.

Get set

Digging For Clay

Lift off the topsoil with a spade or similar tool. Push the spade into the ground to a depth of about 10cm (4in) using the ball of your foot. If the ground is covered in grass, cut a circle into the soil to the same depth and then use the spade to lift off your cut section. You will see that this topsoil is a darker, more crumbly soil which will have plant matter in it. Beneath this layer (you may have to dig slightly deeper), you will find clay, which is usually more orange in colour.

To check if you have found clay, dig out a small amount and touch it: it should feel sticky and smooth, not gritty. Roll this little lump into a ball and then into a sausage shape. If it doesn't crack, you have clay.

Making Clay From Soil

Hunt around for a sturdy stick to use later when mixing the mud. Use the spade to dig up enough soil to fill half a bucket. Once done, pour enough water over the soil to cover it (keeping some back for flushing the sieve clean). Now take the stick and mix the mud, making sure that any clumps are broken down. If you know the soil is free from sharp stones, you can always sink your hands in and squeeze out any lumps.

Next, place the fine-mesh sieve over the second bucket and strain the mud mixture through it. It's best to use a fine-meshed sieve as, while clay particles are very small, grains of sand are slightly larger and can make the clay gritty. Use the remaining water to flush as much soil as possible through the sieve. All the stones and plant material left in the sieve can be placed back in the ground from where they came. You can repeat the sieving stage if you feel it will clear out any remaining sand, etc.

Pour the mud mixture into the clear container. If filling a 5l (1 gallon) water bottle, use the funnel when pouring the mixture. There will be fine clay particles in the water; these need time to sink to the bottom of the container, leaving clear water sitting on top of the layer of sediment. This process can take an hour or two – you will see it happening.

Once the clay has separated out, carefully pour off the clear water. Then place your piece of material over a clean bucket and pour the mud mixture into the cloth. Once the mud mixture is lifted in the cloth, the remaining water will drain off underneath into the bucket. The bundle of mud can be squeezed gently to aid draining. When the liquid has been drained off, the clay will be left in the cloth.

Gather up the ends of the cloth and tie them together with string. (Be careful not to let the mixture fall into the bucket.) The bundle now needs to be hung out to dry.

Depending on the water content and the heat of the day, drying can take between three hours to a day. While you're waiting, it could be fun to play a few games, tell stories or have a picnic. When your bundle is finally dry, take it down from where it was being hung so you can use it while it still feels moist.

Go!

Grab a chunk of clay and mould it into your chosen shape. You might want to make an animal that's found in your local area. At our Forest School sessions, we see many wonderful clay animals, including snakes, mice with big ears and hedgehogs with sticks for spines. Or you may want to make a bowl, or clay beads to string together (for this to work well, remember to make a hole in the middle of each bead using a stick). The choice is entirely up to the maker! Once complete, leave your creation to dry if you have enough time, or place it in a container to take home.

TRY THIS!
River banks are good places to find clay.

Endings

Now everyone has unleashed their inner potter, talk through all the amazing creations and why they chose these designs. Did everyone like the feel of clay; if yes, why? Did they know that clay has been used by humans since prehistoric times? Can they think of any other uses for it? Clay is really good at retaining fluids, so it is used as a natural barrier in places such as ponds, to keep water in, or around landfill rubbish sites to stop toxins seeping out. Clay tablets were the first known writing medium and were used long before the invention of paper. One of the earliest pieces of pottery to be found is a figure discovered in the Czech Republic that dates back to approximately 29,000 BC – astonishing! Just like us, our prehistoric ancestors also liked to make things with clay.

MUD TROLLS FOREST GAME

Deep in the wood dwells a band of noisy Mud Trolls, who love to live deep underground in burrows like badgers and paint themselves with sticky, cool, wet mud. They like to crash about the woods just for fun and, like most trolls, they have an insatiable appetite and will generally eat anything they can get their hands on. However, they are not the fastest or brightest in the land and pose no harm to humans – but they are very competitive and, like bears, can smell food from far, far away!

This high-energy game will chase distractions away as players must focus on their strategies to make it through the forest. It will bring the forest alive in a fun, new way, bonding groups to each other and to the natural space around them. Role play will unleash a new-found confidence and make for many amusing, lasting memories for both trolls and adventurers.

Get ready
Choose an area of woodland with a lot of cover that can provide many hiding places. Mark the boundary of this area with your flags, cones, ribbon or string.

LOCATION	Woodland
AGE GROUP	5 years +
LEARNING ABOUT ...	✣ Independence ✣ being active ✣ strategic thinking ✣ role play ✣ team building ✣ imagination ✣ nature connections ✣ confidence ✣ focus ✣ self-regulation
NUMBER OF PLAYERS	6 +
KIT	⇢ Small boundary flags, cones or brightly coloured ribbon or string ⇢ A sturdy stick ⇢ Water to make mud face paint and to wash after ⇢ Dried beans (like chickpeas/garbanzos), acorns or something of your choice that represents food

The size of the area will depend on how big your group is and how thick the woods or bushes are: a larger group or sparser area will need a bigger boundary. Remember to check the play area for any hazards such as broken glass, trip hazards and poisonous plants.

Get set

Choose who will play the Mud Trolls. Ideally they should include adults or older children who are willing to create a fun atmosphere, for example by providing close escapes for the players and acting the part. It's good to have a few Mud Trolls crashing about the area for dramatic effect but the players should always outnumber the trolls, so a group of 13 could have five trolls and eight players.

When everyone understands the boundary and how to play, the trolls can head off and get dressed for the part. Find a sturdy stick and use it to dig a shallow hole in a patch of bare ground. Pour in the water and mix up some glorious mud. Then the Mud Trolls dip their fingers in it and paint on their troll faces with one or two swipes – or smear mud over their whole face if they want! They may even wish to put some sticks and vegetation in their hair.

Go!

The Mud Trolls can scatter through the forest. Meanwhile, the brave woodland explorers are given four beans as they assemble at the designated starting point. When the game starts, they call out, "Mud Trolls, here we come!" The Mud Trolls can then start to moan and groan and clamber about the woods.

The players should aim to make their way through Mud Troll Forest safely to a chosen exit point. Each time a player is caught by a Mud Troll, they must duly hand over one bean to the troll, then return to the starting point. To avoid confusing the trolls, it's best for caught players to walk outside the boundary to get back to the start.

How much fun is had will depend on the behaviour of the trolls. Instead of simply trying to collect as many beans as they can, the trolls should aim to give the players a hilarious time. Working together to catch the faster players while letting the more cautious through, or reaching out to catch a player, only to fall over at the last point with a loud cry always work well. Children love chasing and a good light-hearted scare. By keeping it cheerful and lively, not only will the children want to return to the forest soon but you'll also have lots of funny stories to tell.

TRY THIS!
If players (especially younger ones) lose all of their beans quickly, they can always be given more to keep the fun going.

Endings

You will need no prompting to talk about how everyone did in the game and what happened. Allow time for this as it's a great team-building opportunity. Ask what they liked about the game and if there was anything they would do differently. When things have calmed down, you could ask everyone if they know what a troll is. Trolls originally came from Nordic mythology and Scandinavian folklore and come in many different forms – some giant and strong yet dim-witted, some small like faeries – but all dwell in natural places. Today, trolls appear in many different stories; can they think of any? *Shrek*, *The Lord of the Rings*, the tale "Three Billy Goats Gruff" and the *Moomins* are just a few. Whether they are friends or foes, trolls seem here to stay.

MUD SLING

Mud Sling is one of those games for when you just want to lark about and have some silly fun. But this simple game also requires skills that, through play, become a joy to master rather than a chore or worry to learn. Throwing muddy missiles at a moving target involves the whole body, including the skills of balance, hand-eye coordination and gauging distance to a target and the power needed to reach it. Knot tying requires patience, focus and memory skill. It's a great ice breaker for new groups and can help those who are nervous about dirt and muddy hands to forget about their doubts and join in!

Get ready

Look around for a fallen log or branch roughly 10cm (4in) in diameter and 25cm (10in) long to act as your target. You can increase the size of the target for younger children, while you can decrease it for older children to make the game more challenging after a few rounds. Use the folding saw if necessary to cut your log or branch to the desired size, or simply use the log as you find it.

If cutting with a saw, an adult should first demonstrate its use. Then, if appropriate, allow capable children to have a go under supervision. Prop the log up against another larger log, branch or tree stump. Kneel down in front of the log (this is a steady position that ensures all limbs are out of harm's way), put a gardening glove on your free (non-cutting) hand and use this hand (and if necessary your knee) to hold the log still. To protect your free (non-cutting)

LOCATION	Any natural outdoor space with clean soil and trees
AGE GROUP	3 years +
NUMBER OF PLAYERS	2 +
LEARNING ABOUT ...	⚘ Teamwork ⚘ gross motor skills ⚘ knot tying ⚘ focus ⚘ self-regulation ⚘ sensory experiences ⚘ freedom ⚘ communication ⚘ nature connections ⚘ being active ⚘ independence ⚘ confidence ⚘ patience ⚘ memory skills
KIT	→ Fallen log (approx. 10cm/4in diameter and 25cm/10in length) → Folding saw → Gardening gloves → String or paracord (approx. 6m/20ft long) → Trowel or similar tool → Bucket for mixing mud → Water

hand, place it roughly 15cm (6in) away from the cutting edge. Saw off the end of the log to create the length you want. It's fine for the log to have small side branches, as these will help to keep the log in place once it's tied up.

Now look around for a fairly low-lying tree branch with enough height that the log can hang from it just above the children's heads. Make sure the limb (and tree) is healthy and strong without any signs of rot such as peeling bark, loss of leaves in the growing seasons or fungi. Check that the ground around your chosen tree is free of trip hazards and that the children can move around under the branch freely.

Get set

You now want to hang your log from the branch to create a swinging target for the mud missiles. The string or cord will need to be long enough to tie around the log using a hangman's noose knot, go over the chosen branch and, using a timber hitch knot, be tied around the tree trunk. (You'll need approx. 90cm/35in of cord to tie this timber hitch knot.) Adults can assist younger children by tying the knots for them if needed, while older capable children may wish to attempt the knots themselves once you've demonstrated what to do, with guidance when necessary.

Use a Hangman's Noose Knot

Tie your string around the log using a hangman's noose knot (which the Elizabethans called a "collar").

First, lay your string or cord horizontally on the floor, with one end of the cord within easy reach (this will be your "working end", the end that you move to make the knot). Hold the working end and

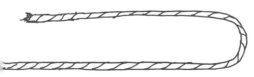

turn it back along the length of the cord to make a U shape that has fallen to the left. This is called a "bight".

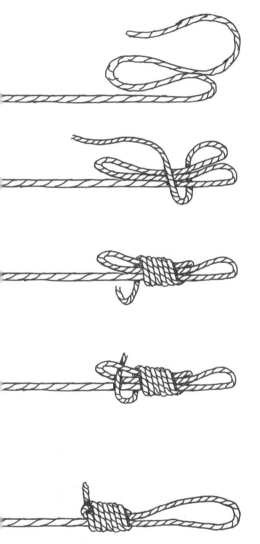

By bending the working end in the opposite direction, create another bight on top of your first one; the cord should now make an S shape.

Pinch these bights together and move the working end underneath and over them all: this is one turn.

Keep wrapping the cord around the bights, making approximately six more turns, and coiling upward along the length of cord.

Once you have finished coiling, there should be a little bit of cord left on your working end. Pass this short working end through the top of the loop near your left hand.

To tighten, pull down on the top of the loop near your right hand. It's this final right-hand loop that you will hang your log from.

Before you place the log in the loop, throw your string or cord over your chosen branch. Once over, thread your log through the loop and tighten the loop by pulling down on the coils. (To untie, simply pull the short working end back through the loop, then pull on both ends of the cord or string to uncoil it.)

Now pull on the free end of the string or cord to hoist the log in the air. Once it is at your chosen height, use the version of the timber hitch knot described below to secure the cord in place around the tree.

Use a Timber Hitch Knot

We will call the section of cord attached to the log and dangling over the branch the "standing end" (1) and the section of cord we will be moving the "working end" (2).

Pull on the working end (2), bringing it down to a comfortable height to work with, and wrap it around the back of the tree. Once around the tree, throw the loose working end over the standing end (1) toward the trunk (this standing end will now be coming down at an angle from the branch to the tree). Now loop the working end (that is around the trunk) three to four times around itself (3). Pull and tighten the knot against the tree. (To release it, slacken the line and unloop the knot.)

Go!

Target in place, it's time to mix those mud missiles. Find a section of earth that's free from any sharp objects, litter and wildlife. Use your trowel to dig up some soil and place this in your bucket with a bit of water. Then mix it to make sticky mud. You will want the mud to form a rough ball so try not to make it too wet. If you are in a clay-rich area, where water doesn't quickly seep away into the ground, you can simply dig a hole to mix your mud.

Roll as many mud missiles as you want; a minimum of five per player is a good starting point. Missiles at the ready, draw a line on the ground that the players must stand behind. Player One now takes their muddy missile in hand. The referee (who is usually an adult, but can be anyone who wishes to perform this role) swings the log. Player One: take aim and launch away! It makes a great splatting sound if you hit the log and feels great. Once Player One has had their go, it's time for Player Two to take aim ... Continue until everyone has used up all their missiles. Oh, and remember – stand clear, Ref!

TRY THIS!
If younger children are struggling to hit the target, try lowering the log, keeping it stationary and moving the start line closer. To make it more challenging, move the start line further away!

Endings

There will no doubt be lots of comments from each player on their slinging techniques, target triumphs and muddy mishaps. You may want to talk about the best mud concoctions for making the muddy balls, or the best throwing techniques. How did it feel to hit or miss the swinging target?

What does everyone think about soil? It may not be the most exciting thing to look at, but it's actually teeming with life. It is often said that a handful of soil has more living organisms in it than there are people on planet Earth. For example, 1g of fertile soil can contain up to one billion bacteria. Can anyone think of any animals that live in the soil? One example is earthworms, which are vital in maintaining soil structure and soil health. As they burrow they aerate the soil and improve drainage. They eat plant material and by doing so release nutrients back into the soil for plants and other organisms to use. Worm castings (or worm poop) excreted in the soil are considered a slow-release fertilizer packed full of nutrients. When underground they eat small microorganisms like bacteria and fungi. They themselves are food for many animals, such as birds. It's safe to say, worms, in their natural environment, perform a great service for their local ecosystem.

MUDSLIDE

Mudslide has to be one of the all-time favourite activities at our Forest School groups. After donning their waterproofs, the kids get busy making slippy, slithery mud and are soon hurling themselves down their very own mudslide. It's hilarious to witness everyone trying to clamber back up, feet skidding around, and even funnier to join in. Hours of simple, good, free fun. This activity is a full-on body experience and workout – from feeling the mud on your hands (and face!), to the effort and balance needed to climb back up. It connects you directly to the ground and the shapes of the landscape. It also encourages great teamwork, as you help each other create and traverse the slide, sharing silly, joyous memories. Don't be afraid to get muddy and dive in ... literally!

Get ready

Find the perfect spot. You are looking for a sloping earth embankment that mimics the shape of a playground slide (roughly a 30–40° angle, with the length of the slide approximately twice its height). Make sure there are no ant nests, plants or tree roots

LOCATION	A natural outside space with unvegetated sloping embankments
AGE GROUP	2 years +
LEARNING ABOUT ...	↓ Sensory experiences ↓ physics ↓ creativity ↓ nature connections ↓ being active ↓ gross motor skills ↓ team building ↓ enthusiasm ↓ confidence ↓ risk assessing ↓ sustainability ↓ communication
KIT	→ Clothes that can get muddy → Waterproof jacket/trousers and shoes → Bucket or equivalent container → Water (at least 3 bucketfuls in dry weather) → Bag to carry muddy waterproofs home
OPTIONAL	→ Trowel, spare clothes

that would be damaged from sliding, and, if needed, seek the landowner's permission first.

Get set

Now it's time to inspect the embankment. Check that there are no trip hazards, sharp stones or sharp litter protruding. If you find any objects that need removing, use a stick or trowel (if you have one) to get them out of the way. Next, it's time to put on your waterproofs if you haven't done so already.

Go!

Pour enough of the water down the slope to make a slippy, muddy slide – and then take a ride! Most kids will start by going down the traditional way, sitting on the slope, but those that are more daring can end up sliding head first – along with a friend. The fun is infectious for both the kids and the adults, so don't be afraid to join in. Our Forest School children love it when we do.

Endings

There will be endless conversations about different sliding techniques and tricks to get back up, as well as exciting tales about the daredevils who went down head first. Once cleaned up, you could ask the sliders if there is anything they would do to change the slide, such as more water or less, or a change of angle or height? How did it feel to whoosh down the slide without a care about getting muddy? Can they think of any animals that like to wallow in mud? Why do they think they do it? Domestic pigs and their wild ancestors warthogs, rhinos and elephants are a few examples of animals that enjoy getting muddy. It seems to be comfort behaviour, helping to regulate the animals' body temperature on hot days, warding off biting insects and acting as a natural sunscreen.

TRY THIS!
Save some water to add to the slide later, when the mud can start to get tacky.

BOGOLAN MUD CLOTH PAINTING

Bogolan mud cloth painting is such a creative and fun activity – from mixing the elements and transforming them into ooey, gooey mud, through to designing unique pieces of art. Bogolan is a beautiful handwoven cloth originating in Mali, Africa. It is dyed yellow using the leaves from a tree called n'gallama and painted with bold geometric patterns and symbols using natural dyes. These dyes include a special river mud that is aged and fermented for up to one year in clay pots, which stains the cloth black. The cloth-dying skills can take years to learn and no two fabrics are the same. This simple version is a joy to explore and you, too, will find that each pattern is unique!

By placing earth in a new context, this is a great activity to push past any fears of mud. With no defined outcomes, there is freedom to explore and create different colours, designs and uses. Being up close to and considering other creatures that live in the mud before it's used helps to develop empathy, curiosity, sustainable thinking and a deeper relationship with nature. Displaying and sharing pieces of work encourages communication, confidence and independence, while learning about the origins of Bogolan cloth creates connections to its design and the culture it comes from. Painting is also simply

LOCATION	Any natural outdoor space with access to fresh soil and ideally a watercourse
AGE GROUP	2 years +
LEARNING ABOUT ...	⬇ Focus ⬇ calm ⬇ independence ⬇ confidence ⬇ empathy ⬇ sustainability ⬇ communication ⬇ freedom ⬇ curiosity ⬇ nature connections ⬇ creativity ⬇ cultural connections ⬇ soil science ⬇ sensory experiences ⬇ fine and gross motor skills
KIT	⇢ A sturdy stick, trowel or similar tool for digging and mixing mud ⇢ Two small containers (approx. 0.5l/1 pint) per artist, or to share ⇢ A tarp or similar ground covering to sit on ⇢ Different sized paint brushes and sticks ⇢ Another jar or container for cleaning the brushes ⇢ Water ⇢ Black and yellow food colouring ⇢ An old white t-shirt or cotton cloth (A3-size)
OPTIONAL	⇢ Printouts of Bogolan patterns, string

relaxing and creates a
fun, focused atmosphere.

So dig in and enjoy!

Get ready

Time to gather some soil ready
to mix into mud. Find a spot that is
free from any litter, vegetation, bug nests
and leaves, and dig up enough soil
to half fill a container. We have used sturdy sticks for this stage –
and in some cases just hands – but if you prefer, use a trowel
or similar tool. To make sure we do not harm our little friends,
we always check through the soil and remove them by placing
them back in the location from where the soil was taken.

Get set

Lay down your tarp and place out the paintbrushes, ready for use.
Search the area to look for differently sized sticks you might like to
use for painting, too. Fill a jar or similar container with clean water
so the artists can clean their brushes.

Now to mix up the mud. Add enough water to make a thick mud
paste that can be painted onto cloth but will not run. You can simply
use a stick for the mixing. Once mixed, divide the mud between
your two containers. You might like to experiment by mixing up
different consistencies and then exploring the different qualities
these have when painted. If it is too watery, the paint will be faint.

Add black food colouring to one of the mud containers to mimic that rich fermented mud used in Mali. In the other container, add yellow colouring, which will mimic the special solution of leaves used to dye the cloth yellow. In our Forest Schools, some artists have used approximately 1 tbsp of food colouring to one 0.5l (1 pint) container, although some halve that amount while some might use a little more, each giving different effects. There's no right or wrong here, so feel free to experiment with different amounts of food colouring.

Go!

Grab a brush, some sticks and a cloth – it's time to make your very own unique design. If you have brought some Bogolan printouts with you, these can be used for inspiration. Or simply unleash your creativity, remembering that in the Bogolan tradition the artists paint the background onto the cloth, leaving the design to be the unpainted areas. But this is just a suggestion, so feel free to be creative and follow your instincts.

Once finished, you can hang your designs across a string line to dry if you have one, or leave them to dry in a sunny spot on the ground. The dried mud will fall away, leaving your designed cloth to be displayed wherever and however you choose. A Forest School favourite is to punch holes along the top and bottom of the cloth, then hang it using string from a stick at the top, before attaching a second stick to the bottom of the cloth for weight. It is then ready to be displayed at home or given as a gift. As one boy said, holding up a very muddy colourful cloth, "My grandma's coming to visit from America and she's gonna love this." It was pretty impressive!

TRY THIS!
You can gently rinse off the mud from the cloth
once it's dried, but this will fade the colour.
On the other hand, repeating the process by
painting over the same design, like they do in
Mali, can add deeper colours.

Endings

Allow the artists to display and share their artwork if they wish to, celebrating all the unique pieces. Ask whether they would like to try something different next time, such as a different pattern or different

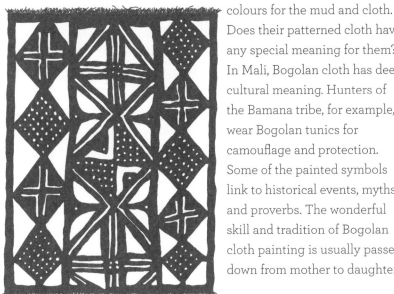

colours for the mud and cloth. Does their patterned cloth have any special meaning for them? In Mali, Bogolan cloth has deep cultural meaning. Hunters of the Bamana tribe, for example, wear Bogolan tunics for camouflage and protection. Some of the painted symbols link to historical events, myths and proverbs. The wonderful skill and tradition of Bogolan cloth painting is usually passed down from mother to daughter.

The Golden Acorn

As morning rose over the village of Pucklehurst, the majority of folk were busy getting ready for breakfast, but not Emory Addison. He was busy tying his shoelaces, getting ready to venture into Wychwood Forest. Emory loved the forest, but the other children couldn't understand why. "You'll be eaten by wolves!" they'd tease. "And there's nothing to see there but mud. Why don't you play football like us?"

Emory was always confused by this; he didn't like football and whenever he did make an effort to play with the other kids, they made him feel like the odd one out. And wolves, well, they had been chased away by farmers years ago.

As he entered the forest, Emory was looking forward to another day of feeding the animals with seeds and nuts, climbing trees, lying back on soft moss-covered trunks and learning about the woodland world. He climbed over twisted roots and pushed past bramble bushes until he reached his favourite spot: an ancient oak tree, the tallest in the forest.

Nestled against the oak's gnarled old trunk, he watched as the leaves fell from the surrounding trees, covering the forest floor with a bright carpet of scarlet, orange and bronze. "What if I was a leaf?" he thought, and he jumped up and dived into the fallen leaves, grabbing handfuls of leaves until they covered him and only his nose poked out.

Bugs crawled across his body but he didn't care. He shifted from side to side, trying to scratch an itch without squishing his forest friends. Something hard pressed into his back. "What's that?" he said out loud. "Doesn't feel like a bug." Finally, he sat up and felt around for the hard lump. "Ah, gotcha!" he said, as his hand landed right on top of it.

He lifted it up and couldn't believe his eyes – a golden acorn glittered in his hand! His heart pounded. Was it real gold? Eagerly checking all sides of his find, he realized it was a living acorn. But how? Shaking with excitement, he raced home to plant it in a pot on his windowsill.

Emory stared at the pot every evening before bed, but no matter how much he stared, nothing grew. Maybe he had been stupid to think the golden acorn would grow.

One day, as Emory wandered as usual toward the forest, his daydreaming was interrupted by the sound of screeching chainsaws. There was a sickening crack that made the ground shake. Emory's stomach churned and he ran as fast as he could to find out what had happened. "No!" he screamed as his eyes fell on the destruction: a whole swathe of trees had been cleared and his favourite tree, the mighty oak, lay smashed on the ground. No one heard Emory wailing over the sound of all the machines.

The villagers told Emory that the landowner next to the forest had been given permission to extend his farm. To Emory, the huge fields where only wheat grew looked like a desert – nothing like the forest that had been home to so many different plants and creatures.

Emory did not leave his bed for the next two weeks. The days grew shorter and winter arrived, bringing with it more rain than ever before – as if the whole world, like him, was crying.

More than anything, he wanted the golden acorn to grow. He held a cup outside his bedroom window to collect some rain, and poured it over the acorn's pot. Still no sign of a tree. He sighed, climbed back into bed and fell asleep.

A strange, gentle, creaking sound woke Emory in the middle of the night. Squinting and rubbing his eyes, he caught sight of a small shape darting through the shadows. "What on earth is that?"

he thought nervously. Turning on the light, he had a terrible shock!

Right in front of him was a tiny tree – and it was alive. The tree had deep green eyes and was jumping up and down, waving at Emory with a branch that had a single golden leaf at the end.

"I've *got* to be dreaming!" Emory pinched himself.

"You're not," said the tree in a high-pitched voice.

Emory gasped. "You can talk?" Still not believing his eyes, he crept slowly toward the little tree.

The tree smiled. "It's me – the golden acorn. Thank you so much for planting me. I'll never forget your kindness."

Emory couldn't stop beaming with joy. His acorn had grown!

"My name is Magus," continued the little tree, smiling with a light that seemed to radiate from his eyes.

In the days that passed, Emory and Magus became great friends. Magus told Emory how trees communicate through their roots and the scent of their leaves. "We share food and sunlight, and we send warnings about nibbling insects. Once warned, we make our leaves taste bitter to repel the nibblers" said Magus, waving his tiny branches around as if sweeping insects to one side.

He told Emory how the whole forest can talk using a sort of "tree internet" made of the tangled, web-like roots of trees and fungus, which can spread far and wide and deep underground. "One teaspoon of forest soil contains several miles of fungal roots or filaments," Magus explained. "Through this underground web," Magus continued, "trees share food and water. And high in the canopy, they give each other space to share sunlight, helping each other survive – especially the mother and baby trees." As if lost in a wonderful dream, Magus hugged himself and began swaying from side to side.

But one morning they both woke to the sound of sirens.

"What's that sound?" asked Magus.

"Trouble," replied Emory, as he made his way to the window. He pulled back the curtains and pushed open the window.

The villagers were frantically throwing their belongings into their cars. Mrs Dimble, who owned the bakery shop next door, was standing in the torrential rain and shaking her head in disbelief as she watched fire engines rush past.

"What's happened, Mrs Dimble?" asked Emory loudly, trying to make his voice reach her over the sound of the sirens and the downpour of rain.

"It's the farm, dear – the one near Wychwood forest," she began in a fluster. "Oh dear, oh dear!" she continued, shaking her head.

"What's wrong with the farm?" Emory asked, slightly annoyed at Mrs Dimbles' dithering.

"With all the rain we've had, the farm has been swept away by a huge flood. All the machines, the house and the crops are all gone – and the landslide is heading toward the village!" she yelled rushing away.

Just then Mr Pinkerton the policeman started banging on Emory's door and hollered, "Grab what you can, we're evacuating the village."

Emory leapt up and frantically started throwing clothes into a bag. It was only when Magus said his name for a third time that Emory paused.

"Emory, stop – I know how I can help!" Magus's eyes seemed to shine with happiness and sadness at the same time. "My roots can hold the soil together and stop landslides. You have to take me to the forest."

Emory scooped his friend up. "That's amazing, Magus!" he exclaimed. Emptying his bag, he carefully placed Magus inside. Then he stopped abruptly and frowned. "But that means you won't be able to walk or talk anymore, right?"

"That's right," said Magus gently. "Once I am rooted, I will join the forest. I will become a tree like all the other trees in the forest."

Emory's vision became blurred with tears. He sniffed and wiped his nose with the back of his hands and rose shakily to his feet. "No, I won't do it!" he exclaimed, and began to pace around the room.

"I can help the village, Emory. I can stop this flood."

Emory swung round angrily. "Why should you?" he yelled. "They tore down the forest – they tore down your family, Magus – they made this happen. They ruined everything."

Magus looked deep into Emory's eyes. "They do not understand what they are doing, their eyes are only half open. It's easy to stay asleep in a nice cosy dream – it's the nightmares that shake us awake. And maybe, just maybe, the nightmare that threatens them now will wake them up."

It was a tricky climb in the heavy rain up to Wychwood Forest, wading through deep, sticky mud and the flood water rushing down the hillside, but Emory finally made it to the spot where the mighty oak had been felled. Here, he gently placed Magus on the ground.

Magus looked at the majestic oak lying smashed on the ground. He picked up a leaf and pressed it to his face and sadness filled his voice. "My roots to your roots," he whispered. Turning to Emory he tried to smile but Emory could see the deep sorrow in Magus's eyes.

"I'm so sorry my people did this," said Emory, a lump in his throat.

Magus's face lit up. "You give hope, Emory. Remember, this is not goodbye, I will be here in the forest waiting for you to visit whenever you can. I will know it's you, just place your hand onto my roots. Now, let's clear this debris away." Magus pointed to where the roots had upturned at the base of the mighty oak.

Emory's legs felt heavy as he reluctantly pushed the leaves, sticks and branches away. Then Magus climbed slowly into the hole left by the old oak. "Stand back!" he commanded. Emory stumbled backward.

Magus reached his branches wide open and a bright golden light shone out. Emory felt its warmth fill his body. Then, as if thunder were erupting underground, the earth shook and wind began to whirl around. Magus grew bigger and bigger, and the golden light grew stronger and stronger, until it burst in all directions – until bang! It was gone.

As the wind died down, Emory stumbled to his feet, not believing his eyes. There before him stood the most magnificent ancient oak tree. "Magus ..." he said in awe. The roots of the tree spread out far and wide, twisting and turning through the ground, fixing the soil in place and breaking the rivers of rain into small trickles that posed no threat.

"You've done it, Magus!" Emory yelled. "You've fixed the landslide!"

The villagers came to learn all about the magical Magus and how the roots of the mighty oak fixed the soil. They learned to share the land with the forest and animals, restoring harmony and balance.

And what of Emory? He never stopped visiting his friend. He would later bring his daughter to the woods and tell her the tale of Magus.

When he grew too old to climb to Wychwood Forest, his daughter came instead, promising to put her hands on the ancient oak's trunk and pass along Emory's love. It was on her first visit alone, as she sat leaning against the trunk of the mighty oak, that she felt a pebble digging into her beneath the soil. Leaning round, she ran her hand over the ground to remove it. "Ah, gotcha!" she said. As she lifted it up, she couldn't believe her eyes – a golden acorn glittered in her hand!

AIR

Air has no fixed shape, colour or smell. We cannot see it directly, but we know it's there. We feel the wind blowing against our skin and see it swaying the leaves and branches of the trees. It catches our kites and carries them high into the sky. We can hear the gentle, low tones of our handcrafted bullroarers as their sound travels through the air.

Air creates our weather, from a gentle breeze to a fierce tornado. And as wind blows across the surface of the ocean, it creates the waves that break on the seashore. Animals, including ourselves, rely for our very existence on breathing in air. We can quickly fill our lungs with breath, to energize ourselves for a fast-paced game, or we can consciously deepen and slow our breathing as we relax in one of our favourite places in nature.

The makeup of our air is unique to Earth and it is essential for life on this planet. The next time you see birds gliding through the sky or an autumn leaf drifting to the forest floor, think of all the glorious things that air does, how we are connected to it and, last but not least, how we can make good use of it on our Forest School adventures!

THE SCREAMING GAME

This game is full of fun and freedom, offering a rare opportunity to run around and screech as noisily as a barn owl. Perfect for high-energy days, when you just feel the need to yell out loud, the screaming game is a joy to play – and it's also hilarious to watch fellow players take their turn. The game will create a sense of enthusiasm for being outside and is a great way to bond a group. It will definitely create some lasting cheerful memories. So line up, breathe in a lungful of fresh air – and go!

Get ready

Adults or the chosen referee should choose a spot in an open area without trip hazards, where everyone can run freely. Set the scene by telling everyone they are going to use the air they breathe to deliver all the oxygen their muscles need to run. Show everyone how to take in a deep lungful of air through their nose, then breathe out through their mouth, making a screaming sound – "AHHH!" – as loudly as they can, until all their breath runs out.

LOCATION	Any natural, open space where noise is not an issue
AGE GROUP	4 years +
NUMBER OF PLAYERS	2 +
LEARNING ABOUT ...	↯ Being active ↯ freedom ↯ self-regulation ↯ team building ↯ patience ↯ nature connections ↯ enthusiasm ↯ independence ↯ confidence

Get set

Select a starting point and ask everyone to line up shoulder to shoulder, facing in the direction they are going to run. Each player will take a turn to run on their own.

Go!

Ask Player One to take in a deep breath of air. Then tap the player on the shoulder and say, "Go!" They can now start running while screaming out all their breath. When their breath runs out – and you'll know as you'll be able to hear them – they must stop, stand still and look back to see how far they've moved with just one breath. Now it's Player 2's turn. Get them to take a deep breath and then tap them on the shoulder as a signal to start running. Work your way down the line until everyone has had a turn.

When we play this game at our Forest School sessions, the children find it hilarious if all the adults join in. I usually end up laughing so much that I run out breath and don't get very far. We often find that everyone wants to play a few rounds, so carry on for as long as you like. For the grand finale, we all run screaming together.

Endings

Players may want to share funny stories about what they saw or how it felt to play the game. For some, it may have been exactly what they needed to release pent-up feelings or energy. Let this stage unfold naturally. You could also talk about how other animals use their breath to run or dive. For example, sperm whales can hold their breath for up to 90 minutes while diving. Cheetahs have extra large nostrils and lungs, adaptations that are needed for an animal that relies on explosive speed to capture its prey. You might also want to tell everyone about *ama*, Japanese free-divers who are famous for diving unaided to depths of 9m (30ft) to collect food and pearls from the seabed. The *ama*, who are usually women, can hold their breath for over a minute whilst vigorously swimming, and some of them continue to dive into their eighties. Incredible! How long could *you* hold your breath for? And how does breathing affect the way you feel? Quick, shallow breathing can make us feel anxious whereas slow, deep breathing can make us feel relaxed as it calms our nervous system. Go ahead and try it some time.

READING CLOUDS

From giant, billowing thunderclouds to thin, candyfloss wisps, clouds come in a multitude of shapes and sizes, offering up a treat for the imagination. Most of us at some point have lain down on the ground and looked skyward to watch them floating by, shapeshifting into fiery dinosaurs, giant bunnies and a myriad of other imaginative things. But have you ever wondered how clouds are made? And did you know that by being able to read clouds, you could actually predict the weather?

We often get distracted by our phones or lost in thought. Cloud reading gets us to stop, look up, to feel the space this action creates and notice our connection to the world. Cloud reading is also a beneficial survival skill, arming us with knowledge that helps us to prepare for whatever the weather throws at us, be that building a shelter from the rain or layering up for snow. No gadgets needed! This activity creates a sense of independence and confidence, as well as endless fun watching those shapeshifting characters in the sky.

LOCATION	Any open space, ideally where you can set up a temporary camp
AGE GROUP	3 years +
LEARNING ABOUT …	✤ Science ✤ imagination ✤ focus ✤ independence ✤ nature connections ✤ confidence ✤ survival skills

Get set

So what are clouds? Adults can explain that, all around us in the air, there is floating water in the form of water gas or vapour. However, we can't see it because the particles are too small and see-through. When the ground is heated by the sun, the water vapour floats high into the sky where it cools down and joins with other tiny objects such as dust to form water droplets. When many of these droplets collect together they form fluffy white clouds. With even more droplets, they turn into grey clouds that become so heavy that the water eventually falls back down to Earth as rain or, when it's cold, as snow, sleet or hail. The shape of a cloud depends on things like the wind blowing it across the sky, air pressure and temperature.

Get ready

Point out that clouds are named for how they look and by where they are found in the sky, or their altitude. Have you seen those low white clouds that look like heaped pillows? They are called cumulus, which is the Latin word for "heap" or "pile".

Low layers of solid clouds that look like flat blankets are called stratus, which is the Latin word for "layer".

White, wispy, hair-like clouds that stretch across the sky are called cirrus, which is the Latin word for "hair" or "curling lock of hair". These are the thin clouds that can be found very high up over mountain tops made of mostly ice crystals and can be seen from an aeroplane.

Alto or mid-level clouds usually look a bit flat and layered as the air at this high altitude doesn't move much vertically. The word "nimbus" also comes from Latin and means raincloud. Other cloud names are made up of two names put together. So a cumulonimbus is a heaped-up raincloud, while a nimbostratus is a stretched-out raincloud. Cirrostratus are high-up, sheet-like clouds that can cover the entire sky. They are so thin that the sun and moon can be seen through them.

TRY THIS!
These are just a few types of cloud. Research more to add to your weather detective knowledge.

Go!

Now you know how clouds are made and what some are called, you can use your nature detective skills to predict the weather.

If it's dry, children can lie on the ground in a clearing and watch the clouds roll by, or they could take a woodland walk to assess the sky glimpsed overhead. First, determine whether you can see the sun through the cloud. If you can, it's a high cloud; if not, it will be a mid-level or low cloud. Then look at their shape: are they stretched out like stratus clouds or heaped like cumulus?

Next, look at how the wind is blowing the clouds across the sky. If they appear to be standing still, a change in weather may not happen for over a day. If they are moving, the weather will change more quickly. Look at their colour: are they white or grey? Scattered, white cumulus clouds tell us it will be sunny, whereas big, dark, cumulonimbus clouds can bring rain, snow, hail and lightning. White cirrus clouds usually mean fair weather but can also let us know a change in the weather is on its way. This change could be from a sunny day to a rainy day. Cirrostratus clouds usually appear 12–24 hours before rain or snowstorms. Stratus clouds let us know it will be a dry, overcast day but if this cloud is thick enough, there will be drizzle, or they can also produce fog. (In fact, fog is actually a cloud you can touch.) With all this knowledge, if wet weather is on the way you'll be well prepared!

For younger children, simply watching the clouds may be wonderful fodder for their imagination. What shapes can they see?

TRY THIS!
Get to know your cloud heights
(temperate regions):

HIGH CLOUD: cirrus at heights above 6km (4 miles)

MID-LEVEL CLOUD: alto at heights of 2–6km (1–4 miles)

LOW CLOUD: stratus at heights less than 2km
(1 mile). A cumulus base can start here, too.

Endings

You might like to get everyone talking about all the animals and shapes that can be seen in the clouds. Does anyone have a favourite type of cloud and why? You could mention that the high cirrus clouds travel at 160kmph (100mph) and discuss how clouds are essential for life on Earth. For instance, at night they reflect heat back down to the earth, keeping it warm, while in the daytime they help to shield us from the sun. Studying clouds helps space agencies like NASA to understand Earth's climate. As we've seen, clouds are linked to the water cycle, bringing both snow and rain. Did you know that the water in a cumulus cloud can weigh the same as 100 elephants? Astonishing!

MAKE A BULLROARER

With a piece of wood, a length of string and the might of our arms we can make music in the air and create a connection to our ancestors and to nature. Found across the world and known by many other names, the bullroarer makes a low droning noise as it is whirled through the air – a sound like a hummingbird's wings. It is both an ancient musical instrument and a way of communicating over great distances.

This activity touches upon so many skills – from identifying the right wood and using tools to carve the correct shape to imagination when decorating the bullroarer. Then patience and perseverence are needed to master its use. It's incredible to see the transformation of solid, earthbound wood into an instrument for making sounds that carry through the air. The whole process brings a wonderful sense of joy, pride, confidence and communication. Magical!

What music will you make and how far will it be heard?

Get ready

First, set up your workspace. Look for a thick fallen branch and a level stump to provide a solid prop for sawing and splitting the bullroarer wood. If you are in a large group, use hazard tape or rope to section off the space for only those who are making the bullroarer.

LOCATION	Woodland (or any natural space if you bring wood)
AGE GROUP	7 years +
LEARNING ABOUT ...	↓ Fine motor skills ↓ nature connections ↓ independence ↓ confidence ↓ risk assessing ↓ tool use ↓ patience ↓ self-regulation ↓ creativity ↓ perseverance ↓ mathematics ↓ tree identification ↓ communication ↓ sensory experiences ↓ focus

KIT	→ A fallen branch and a tree stump → Log (approx. 50cm/20in long) or plywood sheets → Folding saw → Gardening gloves → Pencil	→ Ruler → Froe (if you have one) → Sheath knife → Wooden mallet → Palm drill → Strong string, like garden twine (approx. 1.5m/5ft)
OPTIONAL	→ Hazard tape or rope, permanent marker pens	

Talk through the safety aspects of using a hand-held saw, a sheath knife and a froe if using one. See pages 16–18 on tool safety.

For the bullroarer, you will need to find a rot- and knot-free 9cm (3½) wide log. Your log will eventually be cut to a length of 14cm (5½in). In order to steady the log while sawing to size, look for a slightly bigger log, for example, approximately 50cm (20in) long. As green wood is easier to carve, use fresh, fallen branches if you can. The ideal wood will be slightly dense but also easy to carve, such as ash, sycamore or lime. If cutting directly from a tree, use your gloved, non-working hand to hold the branch. Move the saw in your ungloved, working hand about 15cm (6in) away from your non-working hand (toward the trunk side of the tree) and start to saw. Once demonstrated, an older, capable child can have a go under supervision. Always get the landowner's permission. If a small section of branch has been left close to the trunk, make a final clean cut in front of the branch bark collar or ridge to protect the tree from disease.

TRY THIS!
If you think you won't be able to find a suitable log, you could bring pre-cut plywood, which is easy for younger kids to drill a hole in and decorate.

Get set

You will need to cut a log from your branch to size (14cm/5½in long) before splitting it into a plank. Demonstrate how to cut the branch using a folding saw. Prop your branch up against the branch you have in your work area so that one end is off the floor. Kneel down and use your non-working hand (and if necessary your knee) to hold the lower side of the branch still (the end that is not being cut). To protect your non-working hand, place it roughly 15cm (6in) away from where you will make the cut. Saw off the end of the branch to create a flat, clean surface. Measure 14cm (5½in) back along the branch and repeat. You now have your log.

This time it's the children's turn. If working with one adult per child, the adult should steady the branch while the child kneels down, holds the saw with both hands and saws to the correct length. If you have a group of older children, you can ask two wearing gloves to kneel down facing one another to brace and steady the branch. The third person sawing can grasp the handle of the saw with both hands (no gloves) to cut the log. If working with younger children, it may be safer to hold the branch for them, but watch them closely and judge for yourself.

The next step is to cut a plank of wood from the log. To do this, draw a line with a pencil and ruler along the centre of the log. Now draw a parallel line at a distance of approx. 1cm (½in). Repeat this on the opposite side of the central line to make a third parallel line.

Stamd the log upright on the tree stump and place the froe blade across the central line. With an adult holding the handle, a child can use the mallet to hit the middle of the blade. The log should split in half after one or two blows.

Choose one half of the split log and repeat the steps along the remaining parallel line. The second half of the split log can be a spare or used by someone else.

Assist anyone who may need help. If the froe becomes stuck in the wood, the mallet can be used to hit the end of the blade sticking out of the side of the log.

The same method can be used with a sheath knife. The adult can hold the handle and the child can use the mallet to hit the blade, first on top and then on the blade edge sticking out of the log as it moves down. Just make sure the blade is longer than the width of the log you have chosen.

Go!

It's time to shape the plank into a bullroarer. First, draw an oval shape on your plank.

Remind everyone of the safety rules for using a sheath knife (see pages 17–18) and demonstrate how to use the knife at each stage of the carving process. Carve sitting down, holding the plank in your gloved hand (in a forehand grip) to one side of your body. Cut away from the body and keep the gloved hand away from the cutting edge.

Following your oval drawing, use the sheath knife to whittle the four corners off the plank so it becomes wider in the middle and narrower toward the ends.

A tapered outside edge on the bullroarer will help it to glide through the air. To make this, you need to chamfer the edge of your bullroarer on both sides (cut away the wood to make a symmetrical, sloping edge). Start in the middle and carve toward one end.

Follow the same steps on the remaining edges, then flip over and repeat. You should now have a sharp, tapered edge running all around the outside of the bullroarer.

Next, place the bullroarer on top of the stump in your working area and take the palm drill. On one

end of the bullroarer, drill a hole roughly 1–2cm (½–1in) down from its tip.

For younger children, an adult should hold the bullroarer steady in a gloved hand as the child uses the palm drill to bore the hole near the tip. If older children want to hold their own bullroarer as they drill, let them have a go under adult supervision. Make sure to put the tools safely away after the hole has been drilled.

If decorating your bullroarer, now's the time to get out your marker pens. When you are ready, thread a 1m (3ft) string through the hole and securely tie one end to the bullroarer. (The string can be slightly shorter for younger kids – about the length of their arm.) To attach the string, you can use a double overhand knot. To do this, once the string has been threaded through the bullroarer, cross the short section of string (roughly 10cm/4in) over the remaining long section to make a loop. Then tuck the short end through the loop and pull tight. Repeat again (just on the string this time without going through the bullroarer hole) to secure.

Make a loop at the other end of the string to hold onto when swinging the bullroarer. Again, an overhand knot can be used, but this time double up the string. To do this, fold the free end of the string down along itself about 20cm (8in). Now at the end of this fold make a loop with the doubled-up string around your finger, remove your finger and thread the free end through this

loop and pull tight to create a larger fixed loop. Remember to allow enough string to create a loop that can be easily held.

Now it's time to make music! Make sure everyone stands clear, then place your hand into the loop of your string. Hold on tight and don't let go as you give the bullroarer a spin. Raise your arm and twirl your bullroarer in large horizontal circles overhead like a lasso or vertical circles to your side. When spinning you should hear a low droning sound. To make the sound louder, spin the bullroarer harder; to get a softer sound, spin it slower. By changing the angle and speed, you can create different notes to make your own code. Test how far away the sound can be heard and how you can vary it. What does it sound like to you – maybe a blowfly or a hummingbird?

Endings

The use of bullroarers dates back to the Stone Age. They have been found across the world and have been used in many different ways, including in ceremonies for protection and as toys. They are probably best known today for their use by Australian Aborigines, where the sound would signal something sacred was happening. They're also found in Maori culture where this instrument is known as a *purerehua*. It's name was taken from a moth as the moth's wings in flight sound like a spinning *purerehua*. It's used to call the rains and for communication with other realms and ancestors connecting us all together, but perhaps more commonly today as a musical instrument. Can anyone make up a code or a story with their bullroarer?

WOOD WHISTLE

There's something immensely joyful and satisfying about making a wooden whistle. It's your own unique musical instrument to use however you wish – to alert people to something, play with fellow whistle-makers or sing with the birds in spring. These Nordic wind instruments require you to think about sustainability and tree identification as you gather the right wood, as well as risk assessment and focus while carving the whistle, before finally taking a breath to play.

LOCATION	Any natural setting with goat willow or sycamore
AGE GROUP	7 years +
LEARNING ABOUT …	⬇ Fine motor skills ⬇ nature connections ⬇ focus ⬇ independence ⬇ confidence ⬇ risk assessing ⬇ tool use ⬇ patience ⬇ tree identification ⬇ music ⬇ tree biology ⬇ sustainability ⬇ self-regulation ⬇ perseverance ⬇ mathematics ⬇ listening skills ⬇ sensory experiences
KIT	⇢ One young spring branch (approx. 2–3cm/1in diameter and at least 15cm/6in long) per child ⇢ Loppers or secateurs ⇢ Sheath knife ⇢ Gardening gloves ⇢ Mallet or heavy hand-held log
OPTIONAL	⇢ Hazard tape or rope, tree ID book or app

Get ready

You will first need to find fresh, young (one-to-two-year-old) spring branches about the diameter of an adult thumb (approx. 2–3cm/1in). Look for wood from tree species such as goat willow (*Salix caprea*) or sycamore (*Acer pseudoplatanus*) as their bark will slide off more readily when making your whistle. As always, seek the landowner's permission before cutting wood and, if in a group, talk about the importance of not over-harvesting from any one tree but to spread your foraging across the area. Use clean, sharp loppers or secateurs to cut a straight length of wood about 15cm (6in) long. If cutting whole branches for groups, make a final clean cut in front of the branch bark collar or ridge so the tree can safely heal over. Capable older children can do this under adult supervision, but assist any who may need help.

Get set

Once you have your wood, find a good spot to craft your whistle – somewhere free of trip hazards and with a stump that can be used as a work surface. If you are in a large group, you can section off the workspace with hazard tape or rope for only those who are making the whistles. Talk through the safety aspects of using a sheath knife and demonstrate its use (see pages 17–18).

First, if cutting the branch with loppers or secateurs has caused the ends of your stick to be crushed, tidy them up with your sheath knife. To do this, put the stick on the stump, and rest the blade just past the damaged section. Then use a mallet or heavy hand-held log to hammer down on top of the blade. As the wood is green and soft, it should make a nice clean cut. Repeat at the other end if needed.

Now it's time to rough out the shape of your whistle. Put a glove on your non-working hand (the hand holding the wood). Then measure  approximately two fingers down (3cm/1in) from the cleanest end of your stick, and press your knife into the bark to make a stop cut. You only need to score the wood – don't go halfway through.

Next cut out the start of the air chamber. To do this, come back about 1cm (½in) from the stop cut on the longer side of the stick and then cut down at an approx. 35° angle toward the base of the stop cut. Make sure this cut is nice and clean without frayed edges.

On the direct opposite side of the stick, cut out a simple mouth piece, similar to that found on a recorder. Come down approx. 1.5–2cm (¾–1in) from the tip of the stick, using your thumb behind the blade to guide it, and cut toward the tip at roughly a 35–45° angle. Cut no deeper than halfway through the stick.

At about three fingers down (4.5cm/1¾in) from the air chamber cut, use the knife to score all the way around the stick. A good way to do this is to lay your stick on the stump and roll it away from you while you cut all the way round. Cut deep enough to get through the bark layer but no further than this.

Now it's time to remove the bark. With your knife safely stowed away, place your stick on the stump. Gently tap with your mallet handle around the outer bark without splitting it. (If it breaks you will need to start again!) Tapping will bruise the wood beneath and release sap. You will know when you have tapped the wood for long and hard enough as you will start to see the sap appear at either end of your stick and near the cuts.

You can now separate the outer bark from the wood on the inside of the stick. To do this, hold the stick beneath the scored section with your left hand on top and hold the other end underneath with your right hand. Then twist your hands in opposite directions and you should hear a pop as the bark breaks away. You can now gently push off the bark in one piece. Magic! Keep this tube of bark safe as you will need it later on.

Go!

You can now hollow out the air chamber. This needs to be fairly deep – approximately two-thirds of the way through the stick. To do this, gently and gradually cut deeper into the first stop cut you made, keeping it nice, clean and vertical as you go. Then, as you did earlier, come back about

TRY THIS!
To increase the capacity of the air chamber without weakening it, use the tip of your knife to scrape away the pith.

1–2cm (⅓–1in) from the stop cut and cut down at an angle toward the stop cut. Keep going, gradually shaving more and more wood away. You may need to come back by another 1cm (½in) if necessary until you have carved a deep chamber.

There is still one more cut to do: for the air chamber leading from the mouth piece. The wood leading toward the mouth piece on the same side as your air chamber needs to be shaved away to make a nice, flat horizontal surface. This will make the opening that allows air into the whistle. You may only need to carve away a tiny amount to achieve this. Remember to do this gently – and always carve away from your hands!

Now take the bark sleeve that you previously removed and carefully slip it back onto your whistle, lining up the cuts. Once in place, breathe in – and play your whistle!

TRY THIS!
When carving the air chamber, don't pull off the shavings with your fingers. Always use your knife to remove them carefully. This prevents the wood from breaking and keeps the cuts clean and sharp, which is necessary for the whistle to work.

Endings

It goes without saying that all the makers should spend time playing their unique handcarved whistles. They may want to try different diameter sticks and depths to the air chamber to experiment with different possible whistle sounds. Ask everyone what they enjoyed about making their whistle and anything that they found difficult that could be practised more next time.

Does everyone know what sapwood is? Just a few layers beneath the dead bark of a tree lies the living sapwood. This is where water and minerals are transported between the roots and the crown of the tree. Tapping on the bark of the whistle made these watery sap vessels release their moisture, making it possible to slide the bark from the whistle. Perhaps take a look at the structure of wood – it's amazing stuff! Wood has played a crucial role throughout human history. Besides instruments, can anyone think of any uses for wood? We use wood for fuel, building materials, paper, furniture and much more …

STICK KITES

What better way to connect with air and gain a soaring, birdlike sense of freedom than flying a kite on a dry, windy day? Faces turned upward, eyes locked onto the kite framed by the great expanse of the sky, feeling the tug of the wind ... it's sheer happiness on a string!

Flying a kite gets you active and intricately connects you to your natural surroundings, from sensing changes in the wind's direction to manoeuvring across the ground to keep your kite afloat. Making the kite and overcoming any hiccups along the way also requires patience, perseverance and self-regulation. It can be a therapeutic activity, allowing you to forget about any troubles for a while and become fully focused on accomplishing the flight. There is a beaming sense of pride and achievement as you watch your very own handmade kite take to the skies. Many skills can be mastered as you learn to swoop and turn. And it's a great bonding activity for any group.

LOCATION	Any natural location with open fields and trees
AGE GROUP	4 years +
LEARNING ABOUT ...	↯ Sensory experiences ↯ physics ↯ mathematics ↯ focus ↯ patience ↯ perseverance ↯ creativity ↯ self- regulation ↯ independence ↯ sustainability ↯ freedom ↯ nature connections ↯ fine and gross motor skills ↯ communication ↯ tree identification

KIT

→ Two woodland sticks, approx. 5–7mm (¼in) thick; one 60cm (24in) long and the other 45cm (17in) long
→ Secateurs
→ Ground tarp or blanket to sit on
→ Measuring tape or ruler
→ Pen or pencil
→ 100m (110yd) lightweight nylon string

→ Coloured tissue paper (at least 70cm by 60cm/28in by 24in)
→ Scissors
→ Sticky tape
→ Sturdy round stick (approx. 25–30cm/ 10–12in long and 5cm/2in wide) or a strip of cardboard (approx. 25cm/10in long and 8cm/3in wide) for winder

OPTIONAL

→ Two bamboo canes or wooden dowel rods per kite (if woodland sticks not available), tree species ID book or app, kite line with winding board, ribbon, cardboard work surface (approx. 65cm/25in long and 55cm/22in wide)

Get ready

First, you'll need to find two straight, slim sticks, approximately 5–7mm (¼in) thick, much like a wooden dowel or bamboo cane, one measuring 45cm (17in) long and the other 60cm (24in) long. Lightweight woods include poplar, alder, elder, sycamore and soft woods such as spruce and pine, but in fact most sticks this thickness won't weigh much. Look first to the forest floor to find rot-free sticks; if unable to find any, use clean, sharp secateurs to cut small branches. Adults should demonstrate the use of secateurs and, if necessary, assist younger children. Older kids can cut their own under adult supervision. As usual, seek the landowner's permission first and take only what you need.

To help prevent rot and aid healing when using secateurs, cut your stick back to the main stem of a branch or to another lateral branch along the stem. Be careful not to tear the bark on a living tree. If working in groups, remember to never over-harvest a single tree, and allow the area to recover before repeated use.

TRY THIS!
Make sure your secateurs are clean when cutting from trees, as this helps to prevent spreading disease.

Get set

Next, get comfortable by setting up your workstation. Place your tarp or blanket on the ground with all the tools and materials needed within easy reach.

Your two sticks will form the kite frame. The 45cm (17in) stick will be the horizontal part of the frame. Measure with your ruler or tape and make a mark in the middle of it with your pen or pencil.

Your longer 60cm (24in) stick will form the vertical section of the frame. Measure and make a mark 20cm (8in) from one end. This will be the top of your kite.

Join the marks on the sticks together by placing the shorter stick across the longer stick. At the point where they cross, use approximately 70cm (28in) of the nylon thread – or the length of an adult arm – to tie them together securely.

Use an Overhand Knot:

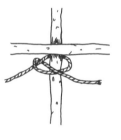

You are now going to use a double overhand knot to tie the thread onto the vertical stick at the bottom of the cross. Take the working (shorter) end of your thread and loop it under and around the vertical stick, coming all the way around so you cross over the top of the non-working (longer) end of your thread. Now tuck the short end through the loop that's been formed and pull tight.

Repeat the overhand knot once more. This time, however, do not take the thread behind the vertical stick but simply pass the working end over the non-working end, push the short

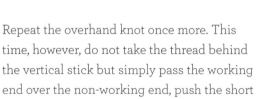

end through the loop that's formed and pull tight. Leave a length of string approx. 10cm (4in) here to tie off the square lash at the end.

Use a Square Lash:

Now use a square lash to secure the sticks together. It can help to think of the crossed sticks as being a compass, with north, south, east and west points. Bring the long end of the string up and over the west side of the horizontal stick and then under the north side of the vertical stick. Then bring it over the east side of the horizontal stick, and under the south side of the vertical stick. Repeat this pattern five or six times, pulling tightly at each turn.

To make the lash even tighter, wrap your thread in between the two sticks – behind the horizontal stick and in front of the vertical stick – about four times, pulling tightly at each turn. This is known as frapping.

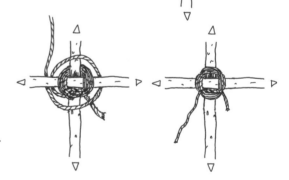

Finish with a granny knot (the first part of the knot you use to tie your shoelaces). Take the section of thread left behind after your overhand knot and wrap it over and under the section of thread leftover from your square lash. Then pull on both ends to tighten. Repeat once more to secure. Cut away any excess string.

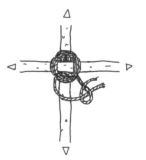

To make the frame really sturdy, run a
length of thread around all points of the
cross. Again, use an overhand knot at
the top of the frame (north) to secure the
thread. Leave a small section of thread here
to tie off the string at the end. Come down
to the right arm on the horizontal stick
(east) and wrap the thread three or four
times around the end of the stick. Move on to the bottom vertical
part of the stick (south) and repeat the wrap. Repeat again at the
left side of the horizontal stick (west). Once at the top again (north),
wrap around a few times and tie off with a granny knot. Place some
tape on top of and beneath your thread wraps to prevent them from
slipping down the sticks.

Go!

Now you need to make the body or sail of
the kite. Lay the frame on top of the tissue
paper, having let everyone choose their
favourite colour. Using a pencil or pen,
carefully make a mark on the paper at each
of the four compass points on the frame.
Now use a ruler to join up the four points.

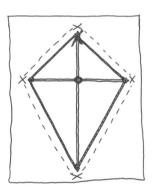

Take the scissors and cut out the diamond shape but remember to
cut wider than the actual drawing, leaving roughly an extra 5cm
(2in) of tissue paper to fold over the kite frame.

When you have finished cutting out the tissue
paper, place the kite frame on top. Now fold the
edges of the tissue paper around the kite frame
and use tape to secure it in place.

Reinforce the top and bottom of your kite by
placing one or two extra pieces of tape across
them. Take your thread and cut off approx.
60cm (24in) and put this safely to one side.

If making your own winder, you can now use a strong granny knot or
double overhand knot to tie the remaining thread onto it. (Make sure
your thread or flying line is long enough to reach high in the sky!)

If using a sturdy stick for your winder, simply tie
one end of the thread in the middle of the stick
and wind the rest of the thread around it.

If using cardboard, and you haven't already prepared it, cut a strip
long enough to hold with both hands and, using scissors, slice a hole
in the middle. You can reinforce this hole and the cardboard egdges
using some tape. Push the thread through the hole and tie on securely,
then wind the remaining thread around the cardboard winder.

It's now time to add the bridle or loop of string that joins the flying
line to the kite. Take the 60cm (24in) piece of thread that you placed
to one side earlier and tie one end of this thread to the vertical stick,
approximately 5cm (2in) down from the top (north) end using a
double overhand knot. Secure the knot to the stick with some tape.

From the top measure 35cm (13½in)
down the vertical stick and tie the other
end of the thread here, securing again
with tape. This string is called the bridle.

For the kite to fly well, the angle of the
kite to the wind needs to be adjusted
for it to catch the wind and produce lift.
This is achieved by hanging the kite
upside down and placing your finger
under the bridle (loop) and sliding
the bridle string over the top of your
finger until the tail end (south end)
of the kite hangs at an angle of
20–30° to the floor.

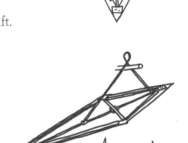

Once this angle is found, pinch the
bridle string together underneath your
finger and tie a small loop here using
an overhand knot.

Securely tie the flight line to this
small loop.

If you wish, you can add a tail made from the tissue paper for
visual effect or to cause drag. This can be 5cm (2in) wide and twice
as long as the kite. Simply cut out a strip of tissue paper and attach
with tape.

When you're ready for your
kite's maiden voyage, find
a friend to help launch
the kite. Work out which way the wind is blowing,
which you can do by sprinkling some grass, a
feather or dry soil in the air and watching which
way it blows: the direction in which it is carried is
downwind. Now ask your helper to stand downwind,
while you move upwind, unwinding your line. Finally,
helper launch the kite – flyer don't let go!

Happy flying!

Endings

Talk over the feeling of flying a kite, and any tips learned for
keeping the kite in the air. You might like to make another kite
that is perhaps bigger or smaller, using different materials for
the sail, such as newspaper or cloth. Some may wish to
practise their knot tying again to master it.

TRY THIS!
**When making kites with
younger children, place
the tissue paper on top of a
cardboard template when
marking and cutting out to
help prevent tearing
the tissue.**

Although the origin of kites is not known,
we know that kites were flown in China
2,000 to 3,000 years ago, and from here
the practice seems to have spread slowly
around the world. Today, there are some
huge gatherings of kite flyers, such as the
International Kite Festival in Gujarat, when
thousands of people come to see the sky filled
with kites, marking the end of winter.

The Mighty Monarch

There was once a kingdom of animals of all sizes and colours, led by the clever and caring King Bear. They lived in peace and were happy except for one thing. There was no wind. The world was so hot without wind, the animals could barely breathe or hunt.

One day, King Bear decided it was time for a change. He called to the animals of the forest, "Who will go to the gods in the sky and ask for wind?"

"I will," hissed Vulture. "I can fly the highest." Off she soared on her majestic wings as the rising hot air took her higher and higher and higher, up into the sky, until the animals could only see a tiny, black dot.

"She must have made it!" yelled Beaver, and all the animals cheered.

Bald Eagle let out a high-pitched whistle and everyone turned to look at him. "No, she didn't," he said, pointing to the sky. And there was Vulture, gliding ever closer until she landed exhausted on the ground.

"I couldn't make it," she gasped. "It was too high and too hot."

Duck stepped forward. "I didn't like to say," he quacked, "but I can actually fly the highest."

Vulture was too tired to argue. "Yes, yes," she said, waving the tips of her wing feathers at him. "Go try! I need the cool wind more than ever."

Duck shook his tail feathers, crouched down and used all his might to leap into the air. Off he went, beating his wings as fast as he could, but it was no good. Moments later he too came crashing back down to earth.

"It's no use," he cried. "What will we do?"

All the animals wailed with despair. Amid the din came a tiny voice. "We could help ..."

King Bear's ears flicked to the side, trying to find out who had volunteered to try, but the complaints and chatter among the other animals were too loud.

"Silence!" he commanded. "Who said that? Who said they could help?"

Eyes darted everywhere but Cougar, Coyote, Otter, Racoon, Moose and many more all shook their heads.

"I did," came the tiny voice. "Down here."

King Bear leant down toward the pink milkweed flowers and saw him – a plump, stripy caterpillar grazing on a leaf.

"You!" roared Racoon and began to giggle. "You don't even have wings!"

Coyote howled with laughter too, and soon all the animals were falling about, holding their sides and chuckling so hard that tears rolled down their hot, sweaty faces.

But King Bear was wise. He had lived for a long time and had seen the magic of these caterpillars: how their colours warn all creatures to leave them alone as they taste foul and are poisonous, and how they can change ... He rubbed his chin while thinking, "Maybe we don't need to disturb the gods"

"Tell me," he said, leaning close to the tiny caterpillar's ear. "How can you help us?"

"You'll see soon enough," said the caterpillar, chomping on a leaf.

King Bear raised his head but all the other animals were still cackling. "The caterpillar will help us!" he bellowed, and bewildered silence spread among the animals.

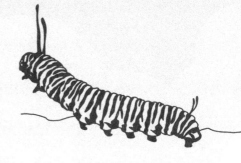

King Bear was never normally wrong but they couldn't see how such an insignificant animal could help them acquire wind.

Days passed by and nothing happened. There wasn't even a caterpillar in sight!

"I think the heat has gone to Bear's head," whispered Coyote to Racoon and Beaver.

"He's surely lost his mind," muttered Racoon, but they dared not question King Bear.

Then one hot morning, King Bear heard the minute sound of cracking. He gathered all the animals, knowing it was time. Racoon and Coyote looked around, trying to figure out what King Bear had announced it was time for.

A few seconds later, hundreds of beautiful butterflies burst into the air, all beating their bright, orange wings together. More and more of them kept coming, until the sky looked as orange as a sunrise. Then it began – the wind from all their beating wings drove the hot air up into the sky and forced cool air down. The wind kept blowing.

Bald Eagle spread his wings to feel the cool breeze lift the heat from his body and all the other animals rejoiced.

"It's time for us to leave now. We head to Mexico for the winter," came the same tiny voice that they had heard before, only now, sitting on King Bear's shoulder was a glorious butterfly.

"But ... but I thought you were a caterpillar!" said Racoon, amazed and peering closer. "You're so magnificent."

"He was once," said Bear, lifting the butterfly onto his finger, "and you are a truly magnificent king of the butterflies. That is why we will call you Monarch," he added, speaking to the butterfly.

Monarch smiled. "I like it!" he said. Flying off to his friends, "and remember" he called back to the other animals: "When we work together we can do anything!"

FIRE

As the Earth orbits the burning sun, the sun's heat fans the flames of life on our planet. With its molten core, bubbling lava lakes and lightning flashing through the sky and setting the land alight, Earth is intricately linked to fire and this element plays a vital part in shaping our world.

Discovering how to harness fire transformed the lives of our ancestors for the better. It allowed them to cook and eat a much wider variety of foods, see in the dark, warm their homes, ward off biting insects and scare off predators. The discovery of fire was revolutionary in the story of humankind.

Today, the ancient art of working with fire is a favourite Forest School activity. It's wonderful to sit around a warming campfire and listen to stories while your imagination drifts with the mesmerizing flickering flames. Cooking foraged food or brewing foraged drinks, or toasting a marshmallow on a stick, offer moments of sheer joy. A fire creates a focal point that encourages a fantastic sense of belonging and community in all who are gathered round. And once the art of making a fire is mastered, there follows beaming pride and an empowering sense of independence. Used correctly, fire is a powerful friend – a vital survival skill. We hope you enjoy this glowing ally and its uses in the following fire activities.

BUG-REPELLENT TORCH

You've found the ideal spot for your camp, but it seems to be the ideal spot for those biting insects too! They are, in fact, just flying around their home environment which you are now sharing, but while you are there you can give them a gentle nudge to move on with a smouldering, handmade bug-repellent torch. Smoke has long been used as a natural repellent for flying insects and it's no wonder, really. Smoke signals fire and fire means danger, making it a place that your tiny friends won't want to hang around in.

Crafting these bug-repellent torches, which use only natural ingredients, taps into many skills. First, you have to focus and connect to the land around you, and identify what you need, including the right fungus (*Daldinia concentrica*), always thinking sustainably as you forage. Constructing and lighting a bug-repellent torch also requires risk assessment, patience and perseverance. Knowing that the land can provide you with what you need and how to use and find these materials will build confidence and independence.

And as for that sense of ease and relaxation once the torces are lit and you aren't being pestered by those infamous mini-munchers … that's priceless!

LOCATION	Deciduous woodland
AGE GROUP	7 years +
LEARNING ABOUT …	↓ Focus ↓ nature connections ↓ sustainability ↓ plant ID skills ↓ risk assessing ↓ survival skills ↓ patience ↓ perseverance ↓ calming ↓ confidence ↓ independence ↓ tool use ↓ being active
KIT	→ *Daldinia concentrica* → Sticks and moss – including one stick approx. 6cm (2½in) in diameter and about 1m (3ft) long; two sticks roughly the width of an adult thumb and approx. 15cm (6in) long → Sheath knife (e.g. Mora or Hultafors round-tip safety knife) → Mallet or heavy hand-held log → Gardening gloves → Firesteel → Fire-resistant gloves → Water to extinguish the torch
OPTIONAL	→ Fungus and tree ID book or app, some previously dried *Daldinia concentrica*, trowel or spade, paper bag

Get ready

First, let's take a look at *Daldinia concentrica*, which is an incredible but often overlooked fungus that grows on dead deciduous trees. Like all decomposers, it provides a valuable service as part of the

Earth's recycling clean-up crew. By breaking down dead wood, it makes the nutrients stored within it available once more to the plants in the surrounding habitat.

Daldinia concentrica is most commonly found on ash trees (*Fraxinus excelsior*), but also occassionaly on beech (*Fagus sylvatica*) and silver birch (*Betula pendula*). Its mature, black, round, fruiting body, which looks like a lump of coal, is the source of its many common names, including coal fungus, carbon balls and King Alfred's cake. It's association with fire doesn't end there. This fungus, once dried, is a useful form of tinder and has long been used for fire lighting. A spark from a firesteel can set it alight and, like a charcoal briquette, it will burn slowly. Its burning embers can be used to transport fires, by placing them in a bundle of tinder that can then be used to ignite a new fire elsewhere. It's this slow burn and the pungent smoke given off that will create our bug repellent.

First, you need to harvest some mature, dry *Daldinia concentrica*. Remember to seek the landowner's permission first. When mature, the fungus is black, dry, light and hard to the touch. If you tap it

gently, it will make a hollow sound without crumbling. It is this stage you are after – not its young, purple-brown stage. If in doubt, use a fungus identification book, website or app. Once you have confidently identified the fungus, think sustainably as you harvest, taking only what you need and spread your foraging out over the area. It's best to pick *Daldinia concentrica* on a sunny day when the fungus will be quite dry. If possible, harvest it under branches, where it will be even drier. Various insects, such as caterpillars of the concealer moth, and other small animals eat or make their home inside this fungus, so cast an eye over the fungus before harvesting to see if you can see any creatures. If you see signs of their presence, leave the fungus alone and choose another instead.

Get set

You can now find the other materials you need for your bug-repellent torch. First, you need to find a stick that is roughly 6cm (2½in) in diameter and with a length of about 1m (3ft) or a length that the maker can easily reach above. Next, gather two sticks that are roughly the width of an adult thumb and about 15cm (6in) long. Make sure all the wood that you gather is rot-free. Finally, gather a handful of moss. Again, take only what you need and spread your foraging out across the area. Check for any of our little forest friends that may be living inside the moss, and either gently remove them or choose another clump.

TRY THIS!
If it's at all damp, fresh fungus may be tricky to light. As a backup to use on site, try drying out some fungus in advance by leaving it in a paper bag on the radiator at home for a few days.

Go!

Before you construct your torches, an adult should explain tool safety and how to handle a sheath knife correctly (see pages 17–18). Explain that the stick will be split into four at the top using the sheath knife and a mallet or heavy hand-held log. To demonstrate this, an adult wearing gloves can hold the sheath knife across the top and middle of the stick. They can use their other hand to steady the stick. An ungloved helper can now hammer on top of the knife with a mallet or log to split the wood to a depth of roughly 15cm (6in).

Once the knife has entered the wood, hammer on the tip of the knife that is sticking out until you reach the required depth. Place your freed knife across the first split, forming a cross shape, and repeat this process, hammering down to the same depth of 15cm (6in). Capable older kids can now have a go using their own sticks under adult supervision. Assist where necessary.

The stick should now be cut into quarters at the top. Take the smaller sticks that you've gathered and push them horizontally into the splits to wedge open the stick's cut quarters.

If the ground is soft, push the stick into the earth close to where you will be sitting. If this isn't possible, use a trowel or spade to dig a small hole deep enough to hold your stick. Now place the stick inside the hole, push the removed soil back into the hole around the stick's base and step on the soil to make it firm. The stick should be secure and steady in the ground.

Now it's time to light the fungus. Using your hands, crack the fungus in two. Once open, you will be able to see that *Daldinia* grows in concentric rings, giving the fungus its specific name of *concentrica*. Place the fungus on a fire-safe, level surface, such as a flat stone or cleared ground, and use a firesteel to set the inside of the fungus alight. (If you are unsure how to use a firesteel, read the instructions in Dakota Fire Pit, page 99.)

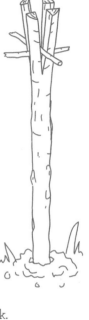

Using the fire-resistant gloves, place the smouldering fungus into a nest of moss and then put this inside the bug-repellent stick. The cut quarters should hold it all in place. If not, you can always pack more moss above and below the covered fungus.

This bug-repellent torch will burn for hours, releasing a pungent smoke that will repel flying insects. If needed, you can always reposition your torch.

Before leaving your site, make sure you fully extinguish the torch by dousing the wood, fungus and moss with water. Touch the fungus carefully and blow on it: if it's cold to the touch and there are no embers, it's fully extinguished and safe to be left.

Endings
What does everyone think of their torch?

Do you know why this fire-starting fungus is called King Alfred's cake? According to the legend, the Anglo-Saxon King Alfred asked a peasant woman if he could take shelter in her home during his battle with the invading Vikings. She granted him his wish on one condition: that he removed the cakes that were baking in the oven when they were ready. Too preoccupied with the conflict, he forgot and the round cakes burned. To hide the evidence, King Alfred scattered them around the forest. *Daldinia concentrica* is said to look like these burnt cakes. And like burnt cakes, these fungi are also inedible.

The next time you see a forest floor carpeted with dead leaves or you come across a decaying branch, spare a moment to appreciate the decomposers for the way they keep nutrients flowing through the ecosystem. Without them, all this waste would just keep piling up!

TRY THIS!
You might like to try adding other dried, natural insect repellents to your torch, such as mint and wormwood.

DAKOTA FIRE PIT

There are countless ways to build a fire, each one having particular benefits for certain situations. A Dakota fire is an underground fire pit. It's thought that this fire lay came from America, where it was invented by the nomadic people who inhabited the plains of the upper Midwest. Tracking herds of bison, they needed a reliable way to create a fire to cook over that would not alert and startle the animals. The fire also needed to be protected from the incessant winds on the plains and to burn without the risk of causing a prairie fire.

With the surrounding soil protecting the flames from the wind, a Dakota fire pit burns extremely hot on little fuel, making it ideal for cooking. It is hidden and, compared to ground-level fires, produces less smoke and little light. It can also be easily filled in and concealed when extinguished. The Dakota fire pit is therefore perfect for survival situations, especially when you want to avoid being seen by others – giving the fire its other name: a stealth fire.

The Dakota fire pit that we make at Forest School can be used for cooking or crafts. Building it takes stamina and patience. Lighting a fire with a firesteel helps to develop fine motor skills and may take a few attempts, thereby developing perseverance, determination and focus – and any disappointment allows the children to practise self-regulation of emotions in a safe and friendly space. Working with fire and tools also teaches risk assessment, which includes that of the environment involved. This in turn connects us to the land and creates a sense of independence and confidence. Once built, the fire is ready to use as you wish – boiling dyed cloth, brewing birch tea, cooking a delicious meal or however you like ... the choice is yours!

LOCATION	A clearing (ideally in woodlands) that allows fire
AGE GROUP	7 years + (younger children can join in with digging the pit and fire use, where safe to do so)
LEARNING ABOUT ...	↯ Stamina ↯ patience ↯ being active ↯ fine motor skills ↯ perseverance ↯ focus ↯ self-regulation ↯ risk assessing ↯ tool use ↯ nature connections ↯ independence ↯ confidence ↯ sustainability ↯ cooking ↯ creativity ↯ community
KIT	⇢ Fire safety kit (see page 19), including fire resistant gloves ⇢ Four sticks approx. 1m (3ft) long ⇢ Cotton wool and Vaseline for tinder ⇢ Dry twigs of different widths for kindling ⇢ Small branches approx. 5cm (2in) thick (or to fit in your fire pit) for fuel ⇢ Shovel (micro or folding shovels work well) ⇢ Gardening gloves ⇢ Firesteel ⇢ 35cm (14in) metal fire grill ⇢ Loppers
OPTIONAL	⇢ Tarp, measuring tape, kindling, wood (for fuel)

SAFETY FIRST
Tree-root fires can occur in very dry
areas and cause forest fires, so please do not
build your Dakota fire pit right next to trees or their
rooting systems. Resinous tree species such as pine are
particularly flammable. As a precaution, you can pack extra
soil around the fire pit to cover up any fine roots seen.
Be aware that ground fires can also happen in locations
with peat soil, so always check that it will be safe to use
a Dakota fire pit in your area. Read the fire safety
section on page 19 and ensure that you have
the landowner's permission.

Get ready

To make a Dakota fire pit, you will need to dig two holes. One hole
will be the actual fire pit and the other hole will form a ventilation
shaft that connects to the fire pit via a tunnel. The ventilation hole
will allow oxygen to flow into the fire; this is necessary as the flames
and heat from the fire will not readily allow oxygen in from above.
It also allows you to blow into the tunnel when you need to add
oxygen to the fire, rather than blowing from above where you could
get burnt.

Find a suitable location (see the safety note above) and place your
tools and fire safety kit nearby. Search around for four sticks that
are about 1m (3ft) long and thick enough for everyone to see easily.
These will be your fire boundary markers. Put them with your kit.

As with all fires, you will need tinder to start your fire and kindling to keep the fire burning until it's hot enough to burn your main fuel: wood. If you haven't brought any along with you, you will need to find some dry fuel to use now.

You will be using your cotton wool and Vaseline as tinder. You can also collect and experiment with other tinder sources, such as dry grasses, dead bracken and fluffy seed heads from plants such as thistles. Dry wood shavings and feather sticks (see page 108) can also act as good tinder. Next, gather dry twigs in different widths, from matchstick size to finger size, for kindling, and small branches roughly 5cm (2in) thick (or that will fit in your fire pit) for fuel.

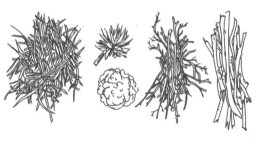

Do not use green (unseasoned) wood as it's hard to burn and can create lots of smoke. You should also avoid painted or treated timber, which will release toxic fumes when burned. Ensure you have enough wood to keep your fire fed and burning for the length of your stay. One of the main benefits of Dakota fire pits is that they need less fuel than ground-level fires.

Get set

Now it's time to get digging! Here, we will be digging a fire pit hole that is approximately 30cm (12in) deep and wide, and a ventilation hole that is about 30cm (12in) deep and 20cm (8in) wide. If you want to make a bigger fire then you will need to dig a deeper and wider hole; you could dig a fire pit that is about 60cm (24in) deep and 45cm (18in) wide with a ventilation hole that is 60cm (24in) deep and 20cm (8in) wide. If you wish, play around with the dimensions. Just remember, if you are using a fire grill this needs to rest safely on the ground above the fire pit – so check its size before digging your hole.

To dig the fire pit hole, score a 30cm (12in) circle in the ground with your shovel. Then start working your way under the turf (if present) and down, removing material as you go to the required depth. Do not scatter the soil you remove, but place it safely to one side for when you refill the holes before leaving. If you want to leave no trace of where you have been, you can lay down a tarp near your chosen spot before removing the earth. As you dig the hole, separate out the different layers of soil onto the tarp as you remove it. Once the fire is extinguished, you can simply return the material back into the ground in the correct order before you leave the site.

TRY THIS!
If the soil is fairly soft, you can dig a Dakota fire pit using just a sturdy stick and your hands!

All ages can help to dig the holes, but younger children may need more guidance and help. If they are using their hands to remove material, check first that the soil does not contain any sharp objects. Gardening gloves can be worn. You can rescue any of the bugs in the pit too!

Dig the ventilation hole about 30cm (12in) away from the fire-pit hole, on the windward side of the pit so it gets a good airflow. To check which way the wind is blowing, have a look at the movement of any clouds or the canopy of trees, or simply feel the breeze on your face. You could also try dipping your finger in water and holding it up in the air; the cool side will be the windward side!

As before, score out the size of the ventilation hole in the ground and start to dig. When you have dug down deep enough, start to dig a connecting underground tunnel across from the ventilation hole to the fire-pit hole. Keep digging until the tunnel is big enough to fit your arm through.

When digging the tunnel, be careful not to break the soil bridge that connects the fire-pit hole and the ventilation hole. Don't despair if your bridge does break: you can fill the gap by laying sticks across where the bridge originally was and then packing soil around the sticks to recreate the bridge.

Go!

It's time to start making the fire. Have all of your fuel to hand and ready to go before you light the fire.

Lay some kindling (dry twigs) across the bottom of the fire pit. On top of this, place some tinder. To make your tinder, gently tease out and fluff up the cotton wool and dab a smear of Vaseline on it. The cotton wool will catch a spark from a firesteel and the Vaseline will help to keep the cotton wool burning longer. If you have collected some natural tinder such as dry grass and seed heads, gather up a bunch of these and make a loose nest. You can then place some prepared cotton wool on top of the tinder nest and put this in your fire pit hole on top of the kindling. Now prepare another bundle of tinder outside the fire pit but right next to it. Tie all loose clothing and hair out of the way.

Next, take your firesteel and ignite the tinder that is beside the pit. To do this, hold the firesteel firmly just above the tinder. For safety, kneel on one knee rather than two when striking, as this will allow you to move easily away from the fire if necessary. With the blade of the firesteel at a 45° angle, strike slowly and strongly along the ferro rod. Always strike away from your body, downward and never toward someone else. This action should produce a spark that will ignite the tinder, creating fire!

Don't be afraid of any sparks landing on your hand as they will not hurt, but avoid sparks near your eyes and be aware of which way the wind is blowing, as it can carry sparks too. If anyone struggles to get a spark, encourage them to stick with it and suggest altering the angle of the striker until it works, assisting where needed.

Once the tinder is alight, take a small stick and push it into the fire pit. This should ignite the tinder and kindling in the hole. Let the small twigs burn, adding progressively larger pieces of wood as the fire gets going. Wear the fire resistant gloves when doing this. Try not to overfill the pit with large sticks but aim to keep the height of the flames level with the ground around the pit. If required, use loppers to cut the wood to size. (See pages 16–18 for tool safety.) Children can help with all of these stages so long as an adult is supervising closely.

Once the fire is burning, put away the fire-lighting kit and place the four long sticks that you found earlier in a square around the fire pit for safety. Tell everyone to keep outside of this boundary unless tending to the fire under adult supervision. When the flames die down, place your fire grill across the top of the fire pit.
The fire is now ready to use. You can always add more fuel if needed.

TRY THIS!
You can control the amount of wind entering the ventilation hole by placing a large rock or stick over the hole to adjust the draft, which in turn will control how fast your fuel burns – a bit like the controls on a gas cooker.

An adult should supervise the fire site at all times while the fire is alight. When you are ready to leave, gently pour water onto the fire, ensuring everything goes out. It's fun to use a stick to mix the ash with water while it stays in the pit before potentially seeping away. Adults can check when the contents are cool to touch, signifying the fire is out. You can now refill the hole with the same soil that you removed earlier.

TRY THIS!
If you have no grill, you can lay green branches across the top of the fire pit to rest pots on. Or you could use a thick, green stick to hang a small handled pot securely over the fire. Always remember to think sustainably and seek the landowner's permission before cutting branches from trees.

Endings

What does everyone think of the Dakota fire pit method? It's not a fire to warm yourself by but fantastic to cook on. If you want yours to be truly a stealth fire, use only the driest fuel and place the largest pieces of wood on the bottom of your fire lay, with the kindling on top. The air will push the gases emitted from the wood through the flames, resulting in less or even no smoke.

Humans have used fire throughout the ages for so many things, such as heat, light and for cooking. Can anyone think of any other animal that uses fire as a tool? Dating far back, people in the Northern Territory of Australia have witnessed birds setting the ground ablaze by carrying burning sticks (created by humans or lightning) to new locations in their beaks or talons. This makes for an easy meal for them, as insects, lizards, birds and small mammals then try to escape the fire. These ingenious birds are called fire hawks and include the black kite (*Milvus migrans*), whistling kite (*Haliastur sphenurus*) and the brown falcon (*Falco berigora*). It gives a whole new meaning to the saying "bird brain"!

FIERY FEATHER STICKS

The art of fire making is one of the most sought-after skills taught at Forest School. The mastery of fire changed our ancestors' lives for the better, opening up a whole new world of heat, light and hot food. None of these advantages are lost at Forest School either, whether we're cooking, warming cold hands or listening to campfire tales. Fire making can be tricky, though, even on dry and warm days – but how about when you need it the most, on those cold and wet days when small sticks may be soaked and even dead wood is dripping wet? This is when feather sticks come to the rescue.

Feather sticks are lengths of wood that are shaved to produce clusters of attached hanging thin curls. Depending on their size, these curls can create the tinder and kindling needed to start a fire, while the body of the feather stick then acts as fuel.

It can take a fair bit of practice to master the art of making a good quality feather stick, as well as patience, perseverance,

LOCATION	Any outdoor location with wood, where fires are allowed if you are making one
AGE GROUP	7 years +
LEARNING ABOUT ...	↓ Patience ↓ perseverance ↓ determination ↓ focus ↓ self-regulation ↓ nature connections ↓ tree identification ↓ fine motor skills ↓ risk assessing ↓ confidence ↓ responsibility ↓ independence ↓ sustainability ↓ tool use ↓ survival skills
KIT	→ One piece of wood per maker, approx. 7.5cm (3in) in diameter and 30–40cm (12–16in) long → Mallet or heavy hand-held log → Folding saw → Gardening gloves → Sheath knife (e.g. Mora or Hultafors round-tip safety knife)
OPTIONAL	→ Tree ID book or app; dry carrier for your feather sticks; if lighting a fire, fire making and fire safety kit (see page 19)

determination and focus. If frustration sets in, the activity offers the opportunity to practise emotional self-regulation in a friendly space. Learning to choose the ideal wood builds connections with nature, tree identification and fine motor skills. Using tools and safely managing fire requires the children to learn about risk assessment. Once mastered, this activity builds confidence, encourages a sense of responsibility and independence, and can result in a welcoming communal fire to share with friends and family. All in all, feather sticks are an amazing survival tool!

Get ready

So what should we be looking for? As with any form of fire lighting, selecting the right material is vital. For a feather stick, that means dry and rot-free wood – preferably sourced from a dead yet standing tree that still has its bark intact. A dead branch that has broken from the main tree but not yet fallen to the ground would be ideal. Try to select pieces of wood that are relatively free of knots, side branches or the remnants of them, as this will make for easier carving. Tree species that work particularly well for feather sticks include cedar, hazel, pine and sweet chestnut.

As we will be using a knife to split the wood into four quarters, the piece of wood must be large enough to be batoned, so select a section that's approx. 7.5cm (3in) in diameter and 30–40cm (12–16in) long. This diameter will also help prevent rain from seeping into the wood.

TRY THIS!
If building a fire, make a couple of feather sticks and cut some selected dead wood into sections to gain all the fuel that you need.

When deciding on your workspace, try to locate a sturdy stump, small fallen tree or flat rock that can be used as a prop when later splitting the wood. If you have no mallet, look for a solid hand-held log you can use for batoning.

Get set

Once you have located an unattached, dry branch, it may need to be cut to size. If so, an adult should first demonstrate how to use a folding saw. Prop the branch up against your sturdy stump or fallen tree to raise the end you want to cut off the ground. This will prevent the saw blade from cutting into the soil and keep the branch dry if the ground is wet. Kneel down in front of the branch; this is a steady position that will keep limbs out of the way of the saw's blade.

Put a gardening glove on your non-working hand and use this hand (and if necessary your knee) to hold the lower end of the branch that is not being cut still. As the blade can sometimes bounce out of the cut, your non-working hand should be roughly 15cm (6in) away from the cutting edge. If you need to, saw off the end of the branch to tidy it up, then move your saw into the relevant position and saw off the necessary length. Remember to try to keep both sawn ends of the wood level and flat, as this will keep the wood steady when later splitting into quarters on top of your prop.

If working with a group of older children, you can ask two of them to put on gloves and kneel down, facing one another, to brace and steady the branch. The third child can then grasp the handle of the saw with both hands (without gloves) and cut the branch at a safe distance from the helpers.

If cutting a dead branch directly from a living or dead tree, place a glove on your non-working hand and hold the selected branch. Use the saw to cut off the branch, but again remember to keep your non-working hand approximately 15cm (6in) away from the cutting edge for safety. If needed, follow the instructions above to obtain your chosen piece of wood. Once an adult has demonstrated how to do all of this, children can try sawing under adult supervision. Assist where needed.

You now need to access the dry wood inside your chosen branch. Do this by using your knife and a mallet to baton through the wood, splitting it into quarters. First, place the branch on top of your prop. An adult can hold the knife handle and place the blade across the middle of the wood.

A child can then use the mallet or batoning log to hit the middle of the blade. The wood should split in half after one or two blows. If not, hit the edge of the knife blade that sticks out of the wood as it moves down to complete splitting. Repeat again on each half of the wood to create quarters.

If the outside of your branch is very wet, you can use the same batoning technique to shave off the outer surface and remove the bark, until you are left with dry wood. Keep the knife handy for the next stage, but stress that all tools must be returned to an adult and stored securely out of the way when they're no longer in use.

TRY THIS!
Once you have split your feather stick, place
the inside cut against your cheek: if it's damp
or cold, it has higher water content and may
not be ideal to use!

Go!

You now have a triangular-shaped piece of wood (one of the quarters) with which to create your first feather stick. You can either stand or sit when carving; see what works best for you. Rest your piece of wood securely on your prop. Make sure this workspace is safe for you (you won't potentially cut yourself), safe for others (it's not near anyone else) and safe for your blade (it's not on top of a stone or flat rock for example).

As always, you will be carving away from yourself and wearing a glove on your non-working hand, which will be holding the top of your wood. Raggedy edges are hard to carve feathers from, so this first stage is helpful to complete – especially for beginners. You will first be aiming to create a nice, even surface, which will then allow you to carve long curls that stay attached to the wood.

With your piece of quartered wood resting firmly in a vertical (or near vertical) position on your prop, take your knife and place it on the wood about 5cm (2in) below your non-working gloved hand. Use the straightest part of the knife blade (which is closest to the handle) to carve, as this gives you more control over movement. Lock your shoulder by stiffening it for strength while you run your blade down the wood, removing any bumps or tears created by batoning. You can cut these shavings off. You may need to turn the blade slightly inward toward the wood when shaving, or, if you're using a flat-bevel knife, rest the bevel against the wood. Keep going until you have a bump-free surface to work on. Make sure to keep the edge on the wood that was created by quartering the wood.

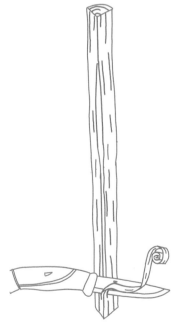

Now you are going to use the same technique to create feathers – curled shavings of wood. Start as you did earlier, by carving from the top of the wood and cutting down toward the bottom. This time, do not cut all the way down as you want these shavings or feathers to stay attached to the wood.

Use the quartered edge to make the first shaving. Then turn the wood left and right as you go so that you are always shaving off the edges – this makes carving feathers easier. Make a nice dense bundle of long feather curls. Try to keep the curls adjacent to each other on the end of one side of the stick, as this will be easier to light. To do this you must start and finish your curls at the same place on the stick each time.

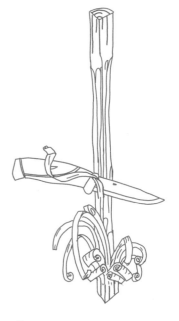

When you are happy that you have enough large curls at the bottom of the stick, make some smaller ones further up the stick that are in line with the large curls, but getting smaller as you move up the wood. Once done, your feather stick is now complete!

TRY THIS!
Put curls on one side of the central curls in order to create a lovely dense bundle of feathers at the end of your stick. To do this, change the angle of your shaving by raising or lowering the tip of your knife as you cut.

Don't worry if you lose some shavings when carving: it happens to everyone! Keep practising, especially on those dry days when a feather stick is not an urgent requirement. You'll get there; in fact, you may even craft a feather stick so beautiful you won't want to burn it!

If starting a fire, shower sparks from a firesteel onto the small feathers. (See Dakota Fire Pit for how to use a firesteel, pages 105–6.)

Once lit, the flames will then light the larger curls and eventually ignite the neck of the stick, which can be used to start a fire.

Endings

Apart from when it's a wet day, in what other situations could feather sticks be useful? They are great in areas where there are no small sticks available to start a fire, such as when camping above the treeline, in sandy areas and at some campsites. Would anyone like to try to carve another feather stick from a different tree species? Remember that hardwoods such as oak, hornbeam and hawthorn are not great for making feather sticks as they are harder to carve. Play around with the angle and pressure of the blade to see what sort of curls you can create. You can also try skipping the first part of making an even surface on your wood and see how different it is making feathers on a raggedy piece of wood. Have fun!

SHADOW STICK

It's often much easier than you think to get lost in the great outdoors – and that can include urban areas too! If you find yourself lost without a map and compass, this activity provides a handy trick that can be used as an emergency navigation method. The shadow stick can determine the cardinal directions of north, south, east and west by using the position of the sun. To create one, all you have to do is place a straight stick in the ground, which acts as a solar navigation tool to track the sun's movement through the sky and the shadow it creates. Our ancestors used the sun and stars for navigation and this clever primitive skill is still used today by some who find themselves going astray.

To use it, you just need to remember a few key facts about the Earth's relationship to our burning star, the sun. As the Earth rotates and orbits the sun, it creates a path that the sun appears to follow in the sky, rising in the east and setting in the west, no matter where we are on Earth. It's this east–west movement of the sun that the shadow stick tracks, helping us to get our bearings.

This survival skill focuses and calms the mind, and directly connects you to your surroundings. It involves astronomy, time keeping and an understanding of cardinal directions. Crafting wooden markers helps to develop fine motor skills and risk management. Constructing a shadow stick takes patience and builds confidence and independence. It's also fun to do on a sunny day when you're not actually lost!

LOCATION	A sunny outdoor location with level clear ground
AGE GROUP	4 years +
LEARNING ABOUT ...	⇣ Focus ⇣ calming ⇣ patience ⇣ confidence ⇣ nature connections ⇣ astronomy ⇣ time-keeping ⇣ cardinal directions ⇣ survival skills ⇣ fine motor skills ⇣ tool use ⇣ risk assessing ⇣ independence ⇣ self-regulation
KIT	⇢ One 90cm (3ft) long straight stick ⇢ One 1m (3½ft) long straight stick ⇢ Three approx. 30cm (1ft) small, straight marker sticks ⇢ Mallet, sturdy hand-held log or rock ⇢ Watch or other timer
OPTIONAL	⇢ Potato peeler (one that is robust and shaped like a knife) or sheath knife (e.g. Mora knife), sturdy gloves, several small rocks or pebbles, compass, string for the second shadow stick method, snacks!

Get ready

First, gather all five sticks you will need. Find them on the ground where possible. For your shadow stick, choose a straight stick with a length of about 90cm (3ft). Make sure it's sturdy and thick enough so it won't break when hammered into the ground. Then find another straight stick that is about 1m (3½ft) long, which you will use at the end to line up along the coordinates made by the shadow stick. You will also need three small, straight marker sticks that are each about 30cm (1ft) long and the thickness of an adult thumb. These will be used to pinpoint three shadow points cast by the main stick. Remember to find a rock or sturdy log to use as a hammer if you do not have a mallet.

Once you have your sticks, find the ideal location to position your shadow stick. It's important to pick a clear and level area so that the shadow your stick casts will not be distorted. Also, choose a spot in which you'll be able to see a shadow clearly. You can test the area by standing with the sun at your back: if it's a good place, your own shadow will be easy to see.

TRY THIS!
If it's a slightly overcast day, use a thicker stick to cast a thicker shadow, which will be easier to see. You can use a short stick to cast a long shadow in winter, when the sun is low on the horizon.

Get set
If the ground is hard, you may want to sharpen the tip of your marker sticks and shadow stick. You can use a knife to do this, or, if the bark is not too dry and hard, you can use a potato peeler. (Peelers work well for younger children and for those who are new to knife skills.) An adult should now talk through the safety aspects of using tools, particularly a sheath knife, and demonstrate how to use a knife and/ or peeler (see Tool Use, pages 16–18).

To form a point on a stick, come back about 2.5cm (1in) from one end of the stick and use the knife (or peeler) to shave off the tip. If using the knife, angle it at approximately 30°, as if you're aiming for the middle of the stick. Start to shave off the wood, rotating the stick as you go. It should end up looking like the tip of a sharpened pencil. Your shadow stick and markers are now ready to use.

Go!

Take your shadow stick and use your log, rock or mallet to hammer it into the soil. Make sure your shadow stick is perfectly upright, not leaning in any direction and secure enough in the ground that the wind will not blow it over. You should now see a straight shadow cast on the ground.

TRY THIS!
Marker sticks are more accurate, but if they are difficult to find or use (especially with younger children), you can use pebbles.

Take one of your marker sticks and hammer it into the ground at the tip of this shadow. This marker stick will now also cast a small shadow of its own. To make sure it's properly aligned, manoeuvre the marker stick so its small shadow is in line with the larger shadow cast by the shadow stick. You now have your first point for navigation.

As the sun rises in the east and sets in the west, this first point marks west. Why is that? As the sun moves east to west across the sky, the shadows it casts move from west to east. Therefore, as we are tracking the movement of the shadows eastward our first shadow point will be west. However, note that if you are in the northern hemisphere the shadow will move clockwise and if you are in the southern hemisphere it will move anticlockwise!

You will now have to wait about 15 minutes before marking your next point. While you wait, perhaps play a game or enjoy a snack.

As the sun moves across the sky, the shadows will also move, so after 15 minutes place another marker, like you did before, in the tip of this new shadow created by the shadow stick. Repeat once more for a third time: this last point will mark east.

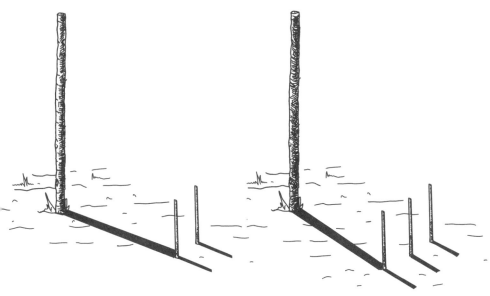

TRY THIS!
If grass distorts the tip of the shadow, move your
hand along the shadow until the tip appears on your palm.
Then lower your hand to the ground and place a stone on
the tip of the shadow in your palm. Slightly lift the stone up
and slip your hand out from under it. Place the stone on the
ground to mark the tip of the shadow.

Now place your 1m (3½ft)
stick along the marker line.
This stick now marks out
your east to west coordinates
and from these you can work
out north to south.

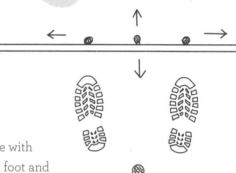

Stand along the east to west line with
the first mark (west) at your left foot and
the second mark (east) by your right foot.
You will now be facing north and behind you will be south. It can
help to use a simple rhyme when trying to work out the direction of
your coordinates. An old favourite goes:

Never (N) eat (E) shredded (S) wheat (W)

We have also heard:
Never (N) eat (E) soggy (S) waffles (W)

Feel free to make up one of your own – they really do help!

If you have a compass to hand, you can check your shadow stick coordinates with it, but remember that the shadows cast from the shadow stick will indicate true north, while your compass will read magnetic north, so some variation between the two readings will be visible.

For the older kids that are really keen to learn more about solar navigation, it's worth pointing out another method, based on the fact that seasonal variation will affect the accuracy of the shadow stick method above. Close to the annual equinoxes, the path of the shadows cast by the sun is close to a straight line, so the shadow stick method is ideal to use in late March and late September, when the equinoxes occur. However, as you can see from the illustration below, when we approach the summer and winter solstices, the path made by the stick's shadow curves – particularly in the early morning and late evening. During these times, the shadow stick method could result in you being some way out on your bearings. Luckily there is a second method that can help, although for accuracy it should be carried out before noon.

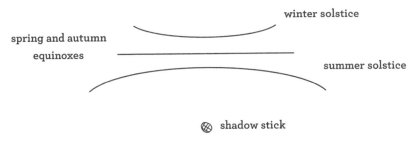

winter solstice

spring and autumn equinoxes

summer solstice

shadow stick

Just like you did in the first method, stake out your shadow stick and use a marker stick to pinpoint the tip of the first shadow that is cast. As before, this first mark is your west point. Now tie a string to

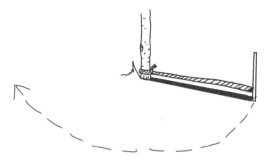

the base of your shadow stick. It may help if someone steadies the shadow stick for this part.

Next, take the string and stretch it out to meet the end of this first shadow. From this point, keeping the string's length the same, draw an arc on the ground, as shown in the illustration above. If you like, you could use pebbles to map the arc or draw in the mud, sand or snow with a stick. As the day progresses toward noon and the sun reaches its highest point in the sky, the shadow will shorten and move away from the arc. As the sun then moves past its highest point and starts to head west, the shadow will begin to lengthen again, and it will meet and cross the drawn arc. Use a marker stick to map when the shadow reunites with the arc you drew. Finally use your 1m (3½ft) stick or draw a line between the first and last marker sticks to create an exact west to east line. Magic!

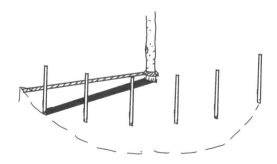

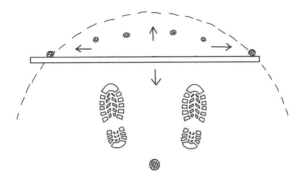

Endings

Have you ever thought about the sun? Its light and heat are essential for life on Earth. How hot and how big do you think the sun is? Well, it's so hot that at its core it is believed to be an astonishing 15,000,000°C and it's so big that it could contain about 1.3 million Earths inside it! Mind-blowing!

What did everyone think about using the sun for navigation? It's believed that our ancestors would have used the sun, stars and planets in the night sky, as well as watched the movement of animals and noted landmarks to guide them. This ability to explore and find our way offered a huge advantage and added to the success of our species. It's still a great skill to have!

Does anyone know when the first compass was invented? It's believed to have been invented in China over 2,000 years ago, but it wasn't used for navigation; the first compass was actually used for fortune-telling and choosing which areas to grow crops and build houses. It was only adopted for navigation many years later, in the 11th century. Prior to that, primitive skills like using a shadow stick would have been invaluable.

FEED THE FIRE

Fire, as we know, needs three things in order to exist: a source of heat, oxygen and fuel. These three form what is known as the fire triangle, and if you take away any one of these the fire will go out. Feed the Fire is a fun, fast-paced game that can instil, in a playful yet focused way, the fire triangle principles. In this game, the players represent the fire and fuel, while the oxygen is all around them in the play area.

Feed the Fire is a great game for burning off high energy, creating a fun atmosphere and acting as a brilliant ice breaker. Playing energetic games can be a helpful way to focus the children's attentions away from any stresses and enable everyone to feel engaged and free through their play. If any uncomfortable feelings arise, it offers a safe space to build resilience. This game also connects players to the environment and creates happy, lasting

LOCATION	Any natural outdoor location where you can run around
AGE GROUP	6 years +
NUMBER OF PLAYERS	5 +
LEARNING ABOUT ...	↯ Being active ↯ gross motor skills ↯ fire triangle principles ↯ independence ↯ confidence ↯ team building ↯ mathematics ↯ nature connections ↯ freedom ↯ enthusiasm ↯ focus ↯ self-regulation ↯ time-keeping ↯ communication ↯ strategic thinking
KIT	→ Thick wool or thread in flame colours: oranges, reds or yellows → Scissors → Timer on a phone or watch
OPTIONAL	→ Small boundary flags, cones or brightly coloured ribbon to mark out the play area, sticks

memories that can develop a sense of custodianship toward the natural world. Dodging trees and avoiding bushes and bumps on the ground help to build stamina and develop physical skills. Time-keeping and mathematical skill also come into play. This is a game that can trigger many debates, and help develop communication skills and strategic thinking – but most of all it's simply good, old-fashioned fun. So fire up and get running!

Get ready

One player (usually an adult but can be an older capable child) acts as the referee and time-keeper. This player can also map out the boundary for the play area, which needs to be big enough for players to be able to run around freely but small enough for the tagger to have a chance of catching the other players. Check and, if necessary, clear this area of any trip hazards or litter that may cause harm, such as glass and dog mess. When explaining the rules, tell everyone where the boundary markers are and to stay inside of them while playing. If you don't have any markers, you can simply point out which boundary landmarks the players need to stay within.

Get set

Gather everyone around and set the scene. Explain the fire triangle principles; how fire always needs oxygen, which is in the air, a source of heat to light it and fuel to keep it burning.

Now set out the game's rules. One player takes on the role of fire. This player can make a circle on the ground with some coloured thread and sticks if they wish to represent a fire pit. The other players will represent fuel; they will be given two pieces of thread each, which they can wear as wristbands, hold or keep in their pocket.

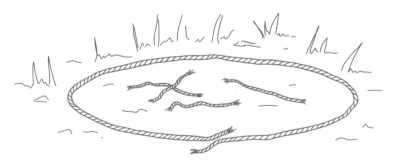

TRY THIS!
To keep the game light-hearted, younger players can be given more lives (in the form of more threads). There could also be more than one fire player. Or, to make it more challenging, older fuel players could have only one life. Experiment and have fun!

Like all fires, this fire needs feeding with fuel. The fire player has to catch the other players by tagging them. Explain that tagging is done with a gentle tap – no shoving or grabbing! Once tagged, the caught player must hand over fuel in the form of one of their threads. They now have only one thread (one life) left. If they lose all their fuel, they come out of the game. The fire player then has to place the fuel threads in the fire pit circle they created at the start to feed the flames and keep them burning. They cannot tag anyone else until they have placed the captured fuel in the pit.

There's one more thing: the fire player is given a time limit of ten minutes to catch all of the fuel and place it in the fire pit. (You can vary the amount of time depending on the size and age of the group and any other considerations.) Each time the fire player catches a piece of fuel and places it in their pit, it adds 20 seconds to the time they have remaining. (As before, you can adjust this time if necessary.) If the fire player runs out of time before tagging and capturing all the fuel then the fire dies and the fuel wins! If all of the fuel threads are collected before the time runs out, the fire player wins!

Go!

Referee, make sure you have your coloured thread to hand (and scissors if you need to cut the threads smaller) and your time-keeping device. Remember to use a stopwatch or note what time the game starts, making sure to add more seconds whenever the fire player puts fuel in the fire pit.

Ask if anyone wants to be the fire player. If no one does or several people volunteer, ask the group to stand in a circle around you. With one finger pointing directly ahead, close your eyes, spin around a few times and then stop: whoever you are pointing at plays the role of fire. If they win the first round, they can choose the next fire player or the pointing method can be repeated.

Once the fire player has been chosen, they can now use coloured threads, or sticks if using them, to set up their fire pit (adults can assist here if needed); a circle with a diameter of roughly 20–30cm (8–12in) will be large enough. While they do this, hand out threads to the other players, who must remain within the boundaries of the play area. At the start, the fire player stands by their fire pit circle. When everyone is ready, the referee shouts out: "Three, two, one – let the game begin!"

TRY THIS!
If in a large group, to avoid confusing the fire player, players that have run out of threads should stand near the referee or, if old enough, stay outside the play area in a safe space.

Will the fire keep burning or will the flames die down – who knows? But this game is sure to keep everyone warm! When the first round has ended, switch players and start again.

Endings

After the first round, the group may
decide to change the amount of
time given to the fire player, so have
a discussion about this and keep it
playful. Players may also offer up
other suggestions for changing the
game. At the end, some may wish to
share funny things that happened, so
allow time for all these hilarious tales.

And why not have another chat
about fire? If you could travel in a
spaceship, on which planets do you think you could build a fire? As
far as we know, Earth is the only planet where fires can burn, thanks
to the amount of oxygen in the atmosphere (21 per cent). But the
Earth's atmosphere didn't always hold so much oxygen. In fact, for
the first half of its history, Earth had no oxygen in the air. About
2.4 billion years ago, this life-giving gas started to appear and we
can thank tiny organisms called cyanobacteria for the dramatic
change. These little microbes invented a clever trick that we now
call photosynthesis, which is how all green plants get their food.
They use energy from sunlight to make sugars out of water and
carbon dioxide, and pump out oxygen as waste. Cyanobacteria made
so much oxygen that this caused the first known mass extinction
on Earth: the Great Oxygenation Event. It was one of the most
important things to ever happen on this planet. Just think – without
it, there could never have been any animals that breathe oxygen,
including us!

Opossum's Tail

An old Mexican Mazatec myth describes how, many years ago, in the time of the ancients, millions of stars glittered in the night sky, setting it ablaze with their fiery lights. The ancients below would raise their faces to the billion pinpoints of light and wonder how they glowed so bright. But as bright as the night sky shone above, on Earth below the ancient people were shivering with cold in the darkness, waiting for the warmth and light of sunrise, for they had not yet befriended fire.

From time to time, one of the stars would explode into life and run across the night sky, pulling its burning tail behind it before crashing to Earth. Using all their hunting skills, the ancients would try to chase these falling stars in the hope of finding one. They believed the stars were messages from the gods which held secrets of the universe that could help the people of Earth. But no one ever succeeded in finding one. Well, almost no one.

There was an old woman known to be a twin spirit – one who had the power to shift from human to animal. There were many twin spirits in the ancient world. Some protected the ancients, while others had no interest in them at all. The old woman was of the latter kind.

She was out one dark night, searching for running stars, when the heavens suddenly lit up with the light of hundreds of stars streaking across the sky. One star shone brighter than all the rest. The old woman stood motionless and focused her eyes on it, making sure to note where it made its explosive landing on Earth.

She held her head still and raised her arms up. Shifting into the

form of a bird, she flew over
rugged mountains, through
misty rainforests and across the
desert, until eventually she found
the fallen star, still burning bright
with the fires of the cosmos.

Feeling the heat of its flames, the old woman took some of the
star's fire back to her mountaintop home. There, she fed it fuel to
keep it alive and, in return, it gave her nightly warmth and light.

Word soon spread of the magical fire. The ancients asked her if
she would share the fire with them. "No," she would say. They pleaded
with her: "Please share your fire!" Some who were brave enough
even tried to steal it, but the old woman guarded the fire well like a
snarling mountain lion and vowed never to share one spark. How
the ancients longed for the warm glow of a fire; they would speak of
nothing else.

One day, Opossum hearing of their plight, came to the ancients
and said, "I will get the fire."

The people were puzzled and began to laugh at her. "But you are
so small, Opossum," they said. "We have already tried and failed.
How will you be able to do something that not even the people of the
Earth can do?"

"I am small but clever and I can climb," said Opossum.
"I shall return with fire."

In the black night, Opossum could see that the old woman had
the fire burning in her house. When she knocked on the door,

the old woman was slow to answer. Opossum said, "Hello, old woman. I am very cold and tired from my travels. May I rest for a while in your house away from the cold night?"

The woman looked at small Opossum and believed she was truly cold. The old woman told her, "Yes, you may enter, but only for a short while – and stay away from the fire!"

Opossum thanked the old woman for her generosity and entered the house. She felt the warming glow from the fire but, fixed by the old woman's gaze, she could not get close to its flickering flames. Opossum sat down. "I have a great trick," she exclaimed, "I can play dead!" Falling to the floor, mouth and eyes open, tongue hanging out, Opossum lay motionless on her side.

The old woman laughed scornfully. "Ha, I can shapeshift!" she declared.

"Shapeshift?" enquired Opossum, rising to her feet. "Can you turn into a snail?"

"No sooner said than done!" The old woman shifted shape into a slow, crawling snail.

Seizing her chance, Opossum leaped toward the fire. She stuck her tail in it and grabbed a burning branch. She ran out of the house, past the little snail, who could do nothing to stop her. Opossum ran across the lands, her tail aflame like the running stars, until she brought fire to the ancients, just as she had promised she would. The people were so happy, they raised Opossum up and sang her sweet songs.

And even today, Opossum walks about with soot-coloured fur and a bald tail, reminding us all of that night long, long ago when she gave the gift of fire to the ancient people of Earth.

WATER

When seen from space, Earth shines blue with its watery surface, and every living thing on Earth needs water to survive. We use this water for so many things: washing ourselves, quenching our thirst, cooking our food, cleaning our homes, creating arts and crafts, building homes and watering crops. Water truly is an essential part of who we are.

Water is a strange, transformative element: it can appear as a solid in the form of ice, as vapour in the air and as liquid in our rivers and oceans. It is always moving through the water cycle. In the form of rain, snow or hail, it falls to the ground. Heated by the sun, it rises again as vapour into the air, where it forms rain clouds and is ready to fall once more.

The elements do not exist in isolation and water, being no exception, is used across lots of Forest School activities. It can be mixed with leaves and twigs to make tasty teas and poured down earthy slopes to make exhilarating mudslides. It is always on hand as a safety measure during our use of fires and helps to wash our hands after playing with mud. Water can be blended with colourful plants to make natural dyes for beautiful works of art. And on hot days, we can have lots of fun with water fights and hilarious water-catching games. So let's dive in and enjoy this incredible element ...

MAKING NATURAL DYES

For thousands of years, dyes have been created from natural materials such as bark, leaves, roots and flowers. A mixture of cooking and chemistry, the alchemy of natural dyes can be unpredictable, affected by everything from the water's pH value (acidity or alkaline levels) to the type of plant used to create the dye. This can result in surprises, especially for beginners – a green plant can create a dye that turns clothes yellow, for example, while a purple plant might turn them pink. And this is all part of the fun. Another natural wonder!

This dye-making activity using ivy involves being focused and following instructions. Dyeing materials is not an instant fix and requires patience and perseverance. Picking ivy calls for plant identification skills and an understanding of sustainability, connecting the participants to the natural world. If something doesn't turn out as expected, that's fine too – it will encourage self-regulation and an open mind. Our Forest School groups simply love this colourful activity with all its transformative magic.

LOCATION	Any natural outdoor space where ivy grows. If using a fire, a site where fire is permitted.
AGE GROUP	6 years +
LEARNING ABOUT ...	⚘ Focus ⚘ patience ⚘ perseverance ⚘ mathematics ⚘ listening skills ⚘ communication ⚘ chemistry ⚘ risk assessing ⚘ identification skills ⚘ nature connections ⚘ sustainability ⚘ creativity ⚘ sensory experiences ⚘ self-regulation
KIT	→ Kitchen scales → White cotton cloth (preferably organic, as natural dyes stick best to natural fabrics) → Natural washing detergent → Stainless steel or enamel pan (for example, a 27l/6 gallon pot will hold about 650g/1½lb of material) → Water (to rinse the pan and cover your cotton three times and simmer for up to 4–5 hours) → Washing soda → Waterproof gloves and a face mask → Long, sturdy stick or long-handled wooden spoon → Stainless steel tongs → Collection pot (one to share or one per person) → Ivy leaves (120g/4oz per 25g/1oz of cotton cloth) → Salt
OPTIONAL	→ Fire safety kit (see page 19) if dyeing outdoors, tarp or blanket to sit on, pen and paper, teaspoons and tablespoons, gardening gloves, scissors, string to make a washing line

Get ready

First, weigh your piece of cotton cloth and make a note of the figure, which you will need later – this is your "weight of goods".

Scouring

Before attempting to dye your cotton, even if it is brand new, you will need to scour or deep clean it. This removes all the chemicals, dust and waxes that collect in the cotton fibres when the cloth is being made and during its transit to the shops. Removing this build-up will help the cloth to absorb the dye and create a nice, even distribution of colour. Older children may like to assist, under supervision, with this stage, which is most easily done at home first.

For best results, prepare your cotton by washing it in the washing machine at the highest temperature on the longest cycle. Use a gentle, natural detergent that's pH neutral and free from bleach and fabric conditioners that might leave residue in the cloth.

TRY THIS!
You can experiment with using different fabrics, such as wool or silk, but do research how to prepare these for dying, as the process varies for different materials.

Once washed, place your fabric in the pan and cover with water. Make a note of how much water you are using, and leave some room at the top of the pan for the water to boil without bubbling over the top.

Next, add 1 tbsp of washing soda for every 5l (1 gallon) of water in the pot, adding the powder to the liquid, not the reverse. Wear gloves and a face mask as washing soda can cause minor skin irritation.

Bring the water to the boil on the hob and simmer for two hours. Using a long-handled wooden spoon or stick, and still wearing your gloves, stir gently from time to time to ensure your cloth is evenly scoured. After two hours your cloth should be scoured of dirt. Allow the water to cool down before removing the cloth safely with your tongs. If the water is very dirty, simply repeat the process and simmer the cloth in more water and washing soda. Next, rinse thoroughly (you can use a washing machine rinse cycle again here if you wish).

TRY THIS!

If you don't have washing soda, why not make your own?
It's really simple! Just heat your oven to 200°C/400°F/gas
mark 6, sprinkle approx. 500g (1lb) of baking soda on a
non-aluminium, shallow pan, and bake for an hour. Stir every
15 minutes to ensure an even bake. You will be able to tell when
it's done as washing soda is more grainy and dull than baking
soda, and it doesn't clump as easily. Once done,
place in an airtight container.

NOTE: if you want to bypass the washing machine, you can place detergent together with the washing soda in the pot with your cloth, using 2 tsp of detergent per 5l (1 gallon) of water. After two hours, rinse both the pot and cloth clean and continue to follow the instructions.

Get set

Gathering Ivy Leaves

If you're not already, it's time to head outdoors! You may want to create your mordant and do the cloth dyeing on an open fire (e.g. a Dakota fire pit, see page 99.) If so, set up your base in a location where fires are permitted and ivy is growing, then build your fire, making sure you follow all the fire safety procedures (see page 19). If you wish, ivy leaves can be gathered while the cloth is being boiled during the mordant stage (described below) as long as an adult stays behind to watch the fire.

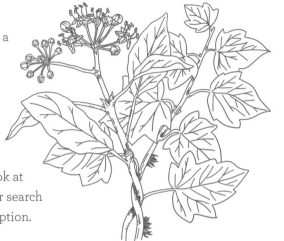

For this dye, we have chosen a plant that grows abundantly in many parts of the world: the shiny, dark-green leafed common ivy (*Hedera helix*). The green leaves should yield a lovely yellow dye. If unfamiliar with the plant, look at a plant identification book or search online for an in-depth description.

Although ivy may be common, it provides a home and food source for many species, so only take what you need and spread your foraging over a wide area. When picking the leaves, it is advisable for anyone with sensitive skin to wear gloves, as chemicals in the sap can cause contact dermatitis. Simply pinch the leaf stalk and break off the leaf, or cut with scissors and fill your collection pot. Using the weight of goods you measured at the start, calculate how much ivy you will need. For 25g (approx. 1oz) of cotton cloth, you will need 120g (4oz) of ivy leaves to give a light yellow dye. For a deeper shade, you may want to pick slightly more.

Create Your Mordant

The next step is to create your mordant – a fixative in which the fabric will be soaked to ensure the dye will stick to the cloth and the wonderful colouring will not fade quickly. There are a lot of mordant options, but our Forest School groups often use a natural one: salt. As a general rule, add one part salt to 16 parts water, filling your pot with enough salted water to cover your cloth and leave room for the cloth to move around. Place the cotton into the water and leave the pot to simmer over the fire or hob for about one hour to allow maximum absorption. When done, carefully pour away the water, rinse the pan and, when it's cool enough to touch, gently squeeze the salted water from your cloth.

Go!

Dyeing

Now place your rinsed pot back onto your heat source and fill the pan with ivy leaves and enough water to again cover the cloth. While the cotton cloth is still wet from the mordant stage, immerse it into the dye bath and bring it to the boil, allowing it to "cook" for one to two hours.

Using tongs to lift the cotton cloth out of the pan, check after one hour to see if you like the light yellow colour. If you would prefer a slightly deeper shade, place the cloth back into the pan for another hour (or longer if you want). Top up the water if necessary to prevent the pan running dry.

Once complete, remove your cloth and hang up from a branch or washing line to dry. Now you can admire the wonderful colour you have created using only natural ingredients.

Endings

Ask how everyone feels it went. Are they happy with the yellow colour they made? Would they do anything different next time? What will they use their dyed cloth for?

How many things do you think produce dyes in the natural world? Dyes can be found in colourful flowers, tree bark, leaves, soil and even food. Food is a great source to experiment with, as you can use leftovers and scraps. For example, avocado peels and pits make a pale pink dye, onion skins make yellow-orange, black beans make blue, while red cabbage makes purple and spinach makes green. Why not have a go?

SPLASH!

This game is fantastic for those sweltering days when being splashed with water is a welcome relief. It's a wonderful ice-breaker for new groups and, with all the laughs and camaraderie, it's great for team building. Being pitched against the element of water itself, rather than each other, allows everyone the freedom of being themselves and playing just for the sheer fun of it. If anyone does feel upset about any spills, this light-hearted game offers a safe space to explore self-regulation. And strength and coordination come into play as you try not to spill a drop of the precious water.

Get ready

Find somewhere to play, ideally near a water source for quick refills. Ensure the area is free from trip hazards and any plants that can sting or scratch. Fill up a spare bucket with water. Next, choose the order of the first two players, bearing in mind that they will need to be strong enough to lift the weight of a full bucket/container.

Get set

Players can now grab their own buckets and form a wide circle, stretching out both their arms to the players on either side of them so only their fingertips touch. Now fill up Player One's bucket with water.

LOCATION	Any outdoor landscape, ideally with a clean, natural water source or running taps available on site
AGE GROUP	4 years +
NUMBER OF PLAYERS	5 +
LEARNING ABOUT ...	↓ Being active ↓ sensory experiences ↓ focus ↓ gross motor skills ↓ freedom ↓ communication ↓ team building ↓ self-regulation ↓ enthusiasm ↓ confidence
KIT	→ One bucket (or equivalent container) per player and one spare to carry water → If no water is available on site, bring a large container with enough water to fill at least three buckets for three rounds
OPTIONAL	→ Towels to dry off with, a change of clothes

Go!

The players now work as a team and their opponent is the water itself! Trying to make the bucket of water last as long as possible, Player One throws the water into the air toward Player Two, who is standing next in line around the circle. Player Two must try to catch as much of the

TRY THIS!
If the container of water is too heavy for younger players to carry, place them further away from the starting point, allowing for more spills to lighten the load before it's their turn.

water as they can in their own bucket or container, then throw the water toward Player Three. Keep going around the circle until all the water has gone, seeping into the ground or dripping from the players themselves!

Endings
There's sure to be lots of laughs and retellings of the highlights at the end of the game, such as who got the most soaked and who caught the most water! Allow time for this before asking if anyone wants to play again.

Some watery facts to share once you've finished your last game: does anyone know how much water is on our planet? Water covers 71 per cent of the Earth's surface, mostly in the form of salty oceans. Because of the oceans' great depths, we have only been able to explore roughly five per cent of this magical habitat. Imagine how many more species there are to discover.

Our bodies are mostly water too, averaging 60 per cent for adults, and it's essential we rehydrate by drinking fluids and eating foods that contain water. Can anyone think of any other species that drink water? How about trees, which suck up water into their branches and leaves through their roots – although we are still not absolutely clear how they achieve this incredible feat! The water is combined with carbon dioxide and sunlight to make sugars – the tree's very own food – in a process known as photosynthesis.

WATERTIGHT DENS

Building dens is always a favourite activity with our Forest School groups. It's a fun way to develop survival skills, as shelter is one of our basic needs. Some dens are carefully constructed with fallen branches and leaves, while others – like long, circular-spreading holly tree limbs or the large cavities in ancient trees – come ready-made by nature itself. But how secure from the elements are the dens we build? In this activity, the structure itself is put to the test. Once the dens have been built, the architects are invited to sit inside them and wait with bated breath to discover if their den is watertight!

Building dens requires a lot of physical energy and offers children the chance to take responsibility, both by thinking sustainably and by assessing and managing potential risks. As they assess ground conditions, the types of branches to use, how to support the den and the effects of the elements, the children will connect more closely with the natural world. Actions such as working out the position of the branches or the length of cord to use, and who will place it where, help to develop mathematical and communication skills, and encourage teamwork. As the children design their structure and make it secure, considerations of physics and architecture come into play. And once their den is complete, children gain an incredible feeling of achievement, self-reliance and confidence in their own abilities, while welcoming others into their space develops a sense of empathy and community.

Here are some suggestions for how to build a den, but all that's really needed is to teach the children basic skills and safe working practices and then let their own incredible creativity and inventiveness unfold. Just make sure the den is watertight!

SAFETY FIRST
Adults should assist with bladed tools where necessary, allowing capable children to do the cutting under supervision (see pages 16–18 for more on tool safety). You can wear gardening gloves to protect your hands when collecting materials. For ease and to help prevent any injuries, demonstrate how to hold any collected branches by the trunk end and trail the branches along the ground behind you. Keep an eye open for trip hazards, too.

LOCATION	Woodland
AGE GROUP	6 years +
LEARNING ABOUT ...	✤ Being active ✤ gross motor skills ✤ responsibility ✤ risk assessing ✤ independence ✤ self-reliance ✤ self-regulation ✤ mathematics ✤ nature connections ✤ empathy ✤ creativity ✤ physics ✤ communication ✤ sustainability ✤ teamwork ✤ listening skills ✤ architecture
KIT	→ Materials for sample dens: a bundle of small sticks, including a stick with a side branch (which can mimic a tree with a lateral limb) and a Y-shaped stick, leaves, vines, bramble or stinging nettle stems, bark and dry bracken. → Building materials for woodland dens: use only what nature supplies, such as those outlined for the sample dens. → Gardening gloves → A hand-sized stone → A cup → Water (approx. 10 cups per den) to test all the dens and to mix mud
OPTIONAL	→ Folding saw and loppers to cut pieces of wood and stems, string and scissors, a spade to dig holes for den posts and/or mixing mud, a pot (or equivalent container) for mixing mud, a tarp or blanket to sit on

Get ready

If you haven't already done so, adults should gather some sample materials: a hand-sized stone, vines, brambles or stinging nettle stems, bits of bark and dry bracken if available and a bundle of small sticks, including a Y-shaped stick and a stick with a side branch to mimic a tree with a lateral limb. Then, gather everyone around and set the scene. You're in the forest in a survival situation and the clouds are hinting that rain is due soon. You need to use the natural resources available around you to build a waterproof den that can keep you dry and warm. Let's talk about your options. What's the first thing you should do?

Encourage everyone to think about what materials there are for building dens around them. These can include fallen branches and trees, vines, sticks, bramble, bark, dry bracken and leaves. Remember to use only what's on the forest floor and not to tear leaves or branches from living trees. If there is an old, fallen tree trunk, a section of the bark could be used for roofing, but always leave some on the trunk for the creatures that make their home beneath it. If you do not have string, perhaps you could use vines or other fibrous plants like nettle stems or young bramble stems. It is always advisable to wear gardening gloves when foraging for your materials and, again, only take what you need and never uproot whole plants. Think sustainably!

TRY THIS!
It's always a good idea to check with the landowner if the den needs to be dismantled afterwards or if certain tree species should be avoided. Try to leave the environment as you found it.

How about choosing a site? You ideally want the ground to be flat, as this is where you will be sitting. The spot also needs to be free from rubbish, trip hazards and ant nests. If you lean anything on trees, check that they are healthy and suitable for supporting the den. Look at the trunk: is it intact or does it have fungus growing from it, which indicates disease? Look up: are there any toppled trees or dead, overhanging branches that could fall onto the den? If the answer is yes, choose somewhere else to build your den!

Get set

Using the sample materials you've previously gathered, show examples of the different ways to construct a den. Push the stick that looks like a tree with a lateral limb into the ground. Show everyone how, once the tree has been assessed for safety, one end of another branch can be leant against this lateral limb and tucked against the tree trunk, while the other end rests on the ground to create a sturdy support for other branches to be placed against. More branches could be placed on one side of this sturdy support to make a lean-to den, or on both sides, to make an A-frame den.

If there are two trees growing reasonably close to one another, with adjacent lateral limbs, maybe you could build a support between them? Always make sure that the branches you use clear both lateral limbs, so they won't fall on anyone's head! To illustrate this, push two sticks into the ground next to each other to represent two trees. Balance a smaller branch between them. Explain that if they can find trees growing like this, they can wedge a branch between them and test the strength of the branch by pulling down on its highest point. If it stays in place, they can use it for den-making and lean other branches against it.

Now, take the Y-shaped stick and push it into the ground. Explain that if the den builders find a large Y-shaped stick, they should first dig it deep enough into the ground so it doesn't topple over! (They can use a spade to help them here.) Take another small stick and show them how they could prop one end of another branch into the Y-shaped gap and rest the other end on the ground. This will form the frame for their den.

To build a teepee den, take another stick, push it into the ground and lean several smaller sticks against this central stick in a circle.

Point out that the style of the den is up to the maker; they may have other ideas but the finished den must be sturdy and safe.

Next, if you have brought a folding saw and loppers, you can demonstrate how to use them to cut fallen branches to a different, desired size (see pages 16–18 for tool safety). Loppers can cut wood up to 5cm (2in) in diameter. If using the folding saw and working alone, first prop the branch on another branch or log to raise it off the ground and prevent the saw cutting into the soil. A safe position is to kneel down in front of the branch, as this ensures all limbs are out the way. Place a glove on your non-working hand and use this hand (and if necessary your knee) to hold the lower end of the branch still. This gloved hand should be roughly 15cm (6in) away from the cutting edge for safety. Then saw off the end of the branch to the desired length.

When working as a team, two partners should wear gloves, kneel down and face each other to steady the branch. A third person with a saw can then cut the branch using two ungloved hands, always making sure that the helpers are positioned well away from the blade. Adults should supervise and assist where needed.

Using gloves, show how to strip thorns or leaves from bramble and nettle stems. Take your stone and gently bash the stripped stems; this can now be used as string if this is needed to complete the den. Vines are good string too.

What can be used to make the den waterproof? Show the sample leaves, dry bracken, bark and sticky mud, which are all good options. Point out that it's a good idea to place some bracken or twigs over the den's branches for the leaves or mud to stick to. Weaving sticks in between the supporting branches will also

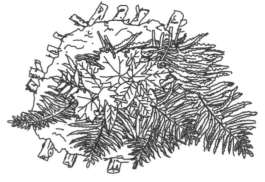

improve the insulation and provide a surface to place the leaves or mud.

Go!

It's time to make the den! Let the builders choose their site, find materials and try out different methods of construction. When the basic stucture is up, enourage the builders to place leaves, dry bracken or mud over the den to insulate and waterproof it.

Once the dens are made, announce that the waterproofing will be tested by pouring cups of water over each den. (You can set a limit here if you wish to – at our Forest School sessions we use about ten cups.) To show confidence in their den, the builders can sit inside it!

Endings

Builders may wish to decorate their dens or make a pretend fire – let their creativity run its course. They may also wish to try out each other's dens. Have a discussion about what methods and materials everyone thinks worked best in terms of waterproofing. Would they change anything if they did this again?

If they were in a survival situation, what else might they need to think about? How about wind direction – it's best not to have the entrance facing into the wind. If the ground is damp, as in mossy areas, how would they make a dry bed? Could they build a raised bed with branches? If they wish to lie down in their den, it would need to be long enough; did they think about this when building it? You can always have another round of pouring water into the dens!

BIRCH TWIG TEA

Foraging for food is so exciting – a fantastic opportunity to tap back into our ancient hunter-gatherer past. As you hunt for tasty morsels, you become fully focused, your eyes scanning the natural world in a totally new way and discovering all sorts of unpredictable things, from caterpillars rolled up in their leaf houses to intricate spider webs and glistening, busy beetles. And then there is the anticipation and curiosity around tasting something new or revisiting a favourite flavour! All connect us deeply to the natural world around us.

Making tea and food to eat from the plants we find around us offers a chance to think compassionately and sustainably. If you uproot a whole plant, you will kill it and thereby take away its chance to reproduce. This leaves nothing for future foraging or other species that rely on the plant for food  and shelter. With this in mind, spread your foraging over as large an area as possible, and never uproot or over-harvest one plant. Follow local regulations about what you can and cannot pick, and, if necessary, check with the landowner first. The plants suggested in this book should be fairly easy to locate and identify, but feel free to do your own research and expand your list of edible wild foods.

This healthy, active pastime encourages us to think about where our food comes from and the amount of time, space and energy needed for its production. It can inspire a desire to cook and find out about nutrition. Apart from learning how to identify a particular plant, it can also trigger an interest in how that plant links to its native habitat and the other species that rely on it. This activity opens up a world of learning, which leads to curiosity, communication and focus, and to feelings of self-esteem and confidence. Finding and making delicious natural food, and knowing its benefits, can also foster a sense of independence as well as food to share!

The graceful birch used in this tea is one of the first trees to unfurl its leaves after a winter sleep and as such embodies spring and new beginnings. Its bright green leaves radiate the freshness of that season – but you can make this brew all year round.

SAFETY FIRST

Positive identification of edible wild foods is vital as many plants are poisonous. Use a field guide or your phone to search for information and pictures of edible plants, and choose wild foods that can be easily identified. Harvest plants in an area where you know there is little to no risk of contamination from pollution. This means avoiding industrial areas, road sides, farmland where sprays are used and dog-walking spots. As with any new food, not all foraged foods will agree with everyone so it's always a good idea to sample a little bit before handling and consuming large quantities. (Unless there is reliable information to the contrary, practise caution and avoid use when pregnant or breastfeeding.)

LOCATION	Any natural location where birch trees grow, including woods, parks, wastelands or gardens
AGE GROUP	4 years +
LEARNING ABOUT ...	↯ Nature connections ↯ species identification ↯ being active ↯ curiosity ↯ focus ↯ self-esteem ↯ compassion ↯ confidence ↯ risk assessing ↯ independence ↯ communication ↯ sustainability ↯ nutrition ↯ community
KIT	→ Tree guide book or app → Birch twigs/leaves → Bypass pruning secateurs → Container for collecting and cleaning twigs → Cold water to rinse the twigs → Two cups per participant (one cup if brewing in a kettle) → Thermos of hot water, or water for cooking on site → Metal teapot (or equivalent) to brew the tea on a fire → Strainer
OPTIONAL	→ Example of what you will be foraging for (e.g. a birch twig), fire safety and fire-making kit if using an open fire (see page 19), sweetener (e.g. honey, maple syrup, sugar or stevia), spoons to stir, additional thermos of hot water to warm steeped tea, 1l (1 quart) Mason jar, blanket or tarp to sit on, something to eat with your tea

NOTE: birch pollen can cause allergies in people sensitive to wild carrot, mugwort, celery, apples, soybean, hazelnuts and peanuts, so if this applies to you it's best to avoid the trees during spring.

Get ready

There are over 50 species of birch tree around the world, so before you head out make sure you are familiar with which one you are foraging for. Here we will be using either silver birch (*Betula pendula*), which is native to Europe and parts of Asia, or black birch (*Betula lenta*), which is native to eastern North America.

Once at your chosen site, use real examples of the tree species or a guide to show everyone what they will be looking for. Explain how they should only take what they need and why it is important not to damage the trees by tearing branches, so they can continue to grow and be available for other creatures to use as food and shelter.

TRY THIS!
If you struggle to find the types of birch trees mentioned here, take a look at other varities native to your area. For example, yellow birch (*Betula alleghaniensis*) is common in northeastern USA, while paper birch (*Betula papyrifera*) is native to the north of the USA.

Get set

If you are making a fire to brew the tea,
you could get this going now. (You
could make a Dakota fire pit,
as shown on page 99.) Make sure
you seek the landowner's permission
and follow the fire safety guidelines
on page 19. An adult will need to stay
and supervise the fire at all times while
everyone else heads off to find a birch tree
(preferably one with a recently fallen branch, as pruning this
will cause no damage). You are looking for a tree with plenty of
of fresh, thin twigs with buds on. You can tell if the twigs are dead as
they will be brittle and snap off. Fresh twigs will flex and can smell
of wintergreen (a mild mint). They will also be green under the outer
bark, which you can check by gently scraping the outer bark away.

Once you've found a suitable tree, demonstrate how to use secateurs
to prune the twigs. (See Tool Use, pages 16–18.) Keep the sharp
blade on top and cut down through the twig onto the blunt part of
the blade. Branches that are larger than the diameter of your thumb
should not be cut with secateurs. Assist younger children but allow
capable older kids to have a go at cutting and collecting the birch in
a container. In terms of quantity, a strong tea will require more twigs
– but start with enough twigs to quarter-fill each cup.

After each pruning session, wipe down your secateurs at home with
warm, soapy water. This will prevent gummy build-up, keep them

TRY THIS!
Xylitol, a compound
obtained from birch trees,
is used in some toothpastes.
So if you're camping
and have forgotten your
toothbrush, you could use
a birch twig as a natural
toothbrush.

clean and prevent the spreading of any potential disease.

Go!

Once you have harvested your twigs, cut them into small sections that are roughly 2.5–5cm (1–2in) long – small enough to fit in a cup. Rinse the twigs clean with water and take this opportunity to also clean your own hands before making the tea.

There are various ways you can make the birch tea – here are a few suggestions for you to experiment with. If you have brought some sweetener along, don't forget to add this to your tea.

If you don't have a campfire, quarter-fill each cup with the rinsed birch twigs and pour over the hot water from your thermos. Allow to steep for 10 minutes (or up to 30 minutes for a stronger flavour), then strain the brew into a clean cup and drink. If you have a second thermos, you can add more hot water to warm up the steeped tea.

Boiling your twigs over an open fire is great fun. Quarter-fill your kettle or cooking pot with twigs, then cover with water. Bring to the boil, then leave to cool before straining and drinking the tea. Alternatively, you can heat the water until it is not quite boiling and then pour over the twigs in a cup, cover and steep as desired, before straining and enjoying. This is the preferred method for some, as boiling the twigs can evaporate the oils that give the tea its flavour and herbal qualities.

You could also process some of your gathered twigs to steep overnight. Choose twigs with up to an average thickness of a pencil. Cut them into pieces that are roughly 15cm (6in) long. Fill a quart Mason jar (or equivalent) with the twigs, then cover with warm (not boiling) water and leave to steep overnight. The water will turn amber or pink in colour and will have a strong flavour. Serve it cold or gently warmed.

TRY THIS!
Birch leaves can also be used for tea. You only need about three young leaves for a single serving. Let the leaves steep in hot water for 10 minutes and then drink.

Endings

Ask everyone whether they liked gathering and tasting their wild tea. Would they like to try different plants and trees? Certain pines, for example, can be brewed into a tasty tea. If you experiment with different edible plants, you could try drying them by leaving them in the sun, or in the oven on a low heat, to drink when they are no longer in season. As dried teas make a stronger brew, remember to use less than you would when making tea from fresh plants. Or how about trying sun tea: leave your chosen brew to steep in room-temperature water, bathing in the sunshine for a few hours.

Birch trees are one of the first trees to colonize open areas, bringing with them the promise of new forests, and as such are called a "pioneer species". Maybe it was this pioneering quality and its shiny white bark that made the silver birch into a holy tree for the ancient Celts, symbolizing new beginnings, light and transformation.

LOG CUP

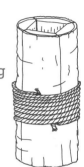

You've headed off into the forest, hiked a long way and now you're dying for a thirst-quenching drink ... You rummage through your bag only to discover you have no cup, nor container of any sort to collect water with. But don't worry! You can easily make your own cup from a log.

Crafting a log cup is a great survival technique and teaches many skills, such as tree identification, woodwork, risk assessment, mathematics and knot tying. Knowing you can make what you need from the environment builds confidence and independence, connecting you to the natural world. This is not an easy task so requires patience, focus and perseverance. Then, enjoy the gasps of amazement when you display your uniquely crafted log cup!

Get ready

First, find a level tree stump that can be used as a stable work surface. If you're with a large group, you may want to section off this work area around the stump with hazard tape or rope, to allow only those making a log cup near the tools.

Now head off to find a suitable branch to make your cup. Remember to think sustainably and take wood from the forest floor whenever possible. If cutting branches from trees, always seek the landowner's permission first. Choose a branch that's as straight as possible, rot-free and without knots. You will need a log that's roughly 15cm (6in) in height and 7.5cm (3in) in diameter for each cup. If in a group, aim

LOCATION	A natural setting with trees, preferably with a water course

AGE GROUP	8 years +

LEARNING ABOUT ...	↯ Tree identification ↯ nature connections ↯ risk assessing ↯ tool use ↯ knot tying ↯ fine motor skills ↯ mathematics ↯ woodwork ↯ confidence ↯ patience ↯ independence ↯ focus ↯ perseverance ↯ creativity ↯ communication ↯ sustainability ↯ calming ↯ survival skills

KIT	→ Straight, knot- and rot-free log, 15cm (6in) by 7.5cm (3in) per person → Gardening gloves for all participants → Folding saw → Pen or pencil → Sheath knife (such as a Mora or Hultafors round-tip safety knife) → Mallet or heavy hand-held log → A reel of paracord, bankline or strong string (allow for a length of roughly 75cm/30in per person) → Water to fill the cup at the end

OPTIONAL	→ Hazard tape or rope, ruler, tarp or blanket to sit on, scissors, strong rubber band for each participant, a tree identification book or tree ID book or app

to select a branch that can produce more than one log. Avoid using wood from poisonous trees, such as yew!

Get set!

An adult should demonstrate how to cut the branch. If cutting a branch (particularly a large one) directly from a tree, you will first need to lessen the weight of the branch, to prevent the bark tearing toward the tree trunk. Adults should demonstrate how to cut the branch. First talk through the safety aspects of using a hand-held folding saw (see Tool Use, pages 16–18). Put a glove on your non-working hand (the one not holding the saw) and hold the end of the branch. Use the saw to cut a section off the end of the branch, keeping the saw at least 15cm (6in) away from your gloved hand for safety.

Now place the saw on the tree-trunk end of the branch at least 30cm (12in) away from the trunk. Using your gloved hand, hold the branch about 15cm (6in) away from the saw for safety. Start to saw off the branch. After removing the branch, make a final, clean cut in front of the branch bark collar or ridge to aid healing and protect the tree from potential disease. If you need to cut more branches from the surrounding trees after this initial demonstration, a capable, older child can have a go this time under adult supervision.

If cutting a branch found on the ground (or a branch already cut from a tree), prop one end on another branch or log to raise the branch off the ground. An adult should now demonstrate how to use the folding saw. Kneel down in front of the branch; this is a steady position that ensures all limbs are out of harm's way. Put a gardening glove on your

non-working hand and use this hand (and if necessary your knee) to hold still the lower side of the branch that isn't being cut. Again, protect your gloved hand by placing it roughly 15cm (6in) away from the cutting edge.

Saw off the end of the branch to create a flat, clean surface on your log. Measure approx. 15cm (6in) along the branch and repeat the process to saw off your log. Now let the children have a go under adult supervision! If working with one adult per child, the adult can hold and secure the branch, while the child kneels down, takes hold of the saw handle with both hands (without gloves), and saws the log to the correct length.

TRY THIS!
If you don't have a pen or pencil to mark your cut pieces of log, you can use a stick dipped in mud.

If working with a group of older children, ask two of them to put on gloves and kneel down, facing one another, to brace and steady the branch. The third child (a safe distance from the helpers) can grasp the handle of the saw with both hands (without gloves) to cut the log. Always make sure the cut surfaces are as flat as possible. If working with younger children, it may be safer to hold the branch for them, watch them closely and assist where needed.

Go!
You are now going to quarter the log. You can do this by eye or draw a cross as a guideline. To do this, on one end of the log draw an even cross on the clean cut surface, using a ruler if you have one.

Now, in your work area, place the log (blank end down) on the tree stuump and put the knife blade across the middle of the log or on the central line you drew.

With an adult holding the knife handle lightly but firmly, a child can then use the mallet or a heavy hand-held log to hit the middle of the blade. Only go to a depth of half the knife blade.

Carefully remove the knife and make another cross-section cut at 90° to the first cut, or along the second line of your drawn cross. This time go all the way through the log. The child can use the mallet to hit the top of the knife and then the blade edge, which will stick out of the log as it moves down through the wood. The log should split in half after one or two blows.

Choose one half of the split log and repeat the steps along the middle score line or drawn line. Repeat again on the second half of the log. This should give you four separate cut pieces. Assist anyone who may need help with this step.

Place the pieces back together in the order in which they were cut. Turn the log upside down and number the cut pieces one to four on what

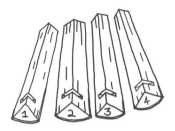

will become the bottom of your cup. This will help you to replace the cut sections back in the correct order when binding your log cup together.

Before assembling your log cup, saw a groove roughly halfway into the split, triangular side and about 2.5cm (1in) up from the numbered end on all four log pieces . Make sure the cuts line up as much as possible as these ends are going to form the bottom of your finished cup.

Next, use your knife to split the inner wood of these four quarters off, all the way down to the depth of the grooves in the same way you split the log. This will form the hollow chamber inside your log to hold the water. You can spend some time after tidying up these cuts with your knife. Adults can do this step or supervise and assist capable children (see Tool Use, pages 16–18). To do this, place the log quarter on top of your stump, hold the top with a gloved hand and use your working hand to shave wood off with a knife. Again, cut down toward the stump and stop at the groove.

When you put the four quarters of wood back together, using your numbers as a guide, you will now have a hollowed-out cavity, just like a cup! Ask someone to hold the pieces of the log together or you can keep them in position with a strong rubber band for the next step.

Make sure your paracord or strong string is long enough to wrap around the log cup several times to fasten the four pieces together. Make a loop in the cord in the shape of a tight U and place it midway on the outside of the log cup. The standing end (short end) of the cord should be on the left and the working end (long end) should be on the right.

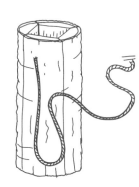

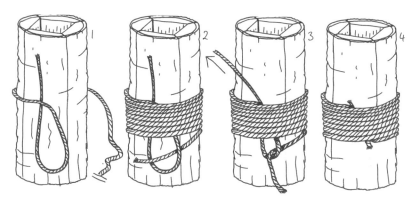

1 Hold the loop in position against the log and wrap the working end of the cord all the way around the log to the left, over and around this loop.

2 Continue wrapping the cord around the log, leaving a short length of the cord at the top of the loop on the left side uncovered, as well as the bottom of the loop uncovered. Once you have gone around the log cup several times and worked your way down the length of the loop, feed the working end of the cord through the bottom of the loop.

3 Pull on the standing end of the cord sticking out at the top to tighten this lashing. Stop pulling when the loop is halfway up behind the wraps.

4 Check there are no gaps in your cup by holding it up to the sky and looking into the chamber. Tighten the cord again if necessary. Now cut both ends of the remaining cord flush with the cord wrapped around the log. The cup is now complete!

Endings

Ask everyone how it feels to have made their very own cup. Did anyone find anything tricky about making it? Would they like to change anything about their cup, such as decorate it? Would they like to test how it works by pouring some water into it? Remind them that it will leak slightly as water always wants to find the easiest route to flow and the log cup will have some gaps in it, so not to worry if this happens.

Drinking water is essential for our survival. A human can only last for a few days without it. What does everyone think we need water for? We need water for so many things: it regulates our body temperature, carries nutrients and oxygen to all the cells in our body and helps lubricate our joints, keeping them nice and flexible. These are just a few of the amazing ways in which water helps our bodies. So fill up your cups and take a big sip!

TRY THIS!
If you submerge your log cup in water for a few hours the wood will absorb some water and expand, helping to seal any previous leaky gaps.

The Water Goddess

An ancient Cambodian myth tells how, long ago, deep in the thick forest, there lived a wise and powerful hermit called Lok Ta. Famous across the land for his skills in magic, he was kind and generous and loved to share his knowledge.

Lok Ta had two devoted students: Moni Mekhala, the goddess of water, and Ream Eyso, the giant storm demon. Lok Ta wanted to offer a treasured gift to his most deserving student, but it was difficult for him to judge who was the most worthy. He decided to challenge his two students to a contest to find out. Handing each of them an empty vessel, he said, "Whoever returns first with their vessel full of morning dew will be master of a magical prize."

Both of his students wanted to please the hermit and earn his respect, and both were keen to win the prize. Ream Eyso thought he had a brilliant idea, sure to win him the honour of being the best, most deserving student. "I'll begin first thing in the morning," he thought to himself and headed off into the forest.

When dawn came, Ream Eyso started collecting dew, carefully shaking all the droplets from leaves and blades of grass into his vessel, until drip by drip the vessel was full. Eager to show his teacher he had won, he headed swiftly back to Lok Ta's wooden shelter. Upon arrival he saw Moni Mekhala already sitting with Lok Ta, her vessel full of dew.

Moni Mekhala, the water goddess, understood water and so had taken a different approach. She had laid out her scarf on the grass overnight. The following morning, she found, as she had predicted, her scalf was wet with morning dew. Wringing out the dew-soaked scarf with one twist, she quickly filled the vessel and presented it to her teacher.

The hermit was pleased with Moni Mekhala's ingenuity and initiative, and declared her the winner of the contest. Lok Ta took Moni Mekhala's morning dew and fashioned it into a beautiful crystal ball, unlike anything found on Earth. It sparkled in the morning sun, glowing with possibilities. As he gave it to her, Lok Ta explained that the crystal ball was very powerful, capable of helping her achieve many wonderful deeds. Thanking her teacher, Moni Mekhala vowed to keep it safe.

Being a kind and generous person and seeing Ream Eyso's

disappointment, Lok Ta took Ream Eyso's dew and fashioned it into a mighty, glittering jewelled axe. Yet Ream Eyso soon grew envious. "Surely I should have been the winner and the owner of the powerful crystal ball," he thought.

Driven by his greedy desire for the crystal ball, Ream Eyso pursued Moni Mekhala and found her dancing in the heavens. He tried to flatter the water goddess in the hope that this distraction would hide his reaching hand, which was creeping closer and closer to the magic ball. But wise to his trickery, Moni Mekhala took flight into the sky.

Full of rage, Ream Eyso chased after the goddess, determined now to take the crystal ball by force. He searched and searched the heavens until he finally found Moni Mekhala. "Give me the crystal ball," he demanded, "or prepare to die!"

The water goddess kept her composure and quietly pulled the ball closer to herself. In desperation and burning anger, the storm demon demanded again, "Give me the crystal ball!" Still the goddess stood fast.

Ream Eyso brandished his new axe, ready to take aim at the goddess. But before he could throw it, Moni Mekhala tossed the sparkling crystal ball high into the air. It hurled through the sky, emitting bolts of lightning that blinded the storm demon. As he staggered backward, unable to see, Ream Eyso flung his axe in one final attempt to defeat Moni Mekhala. When it cut through the clouds, the impact was so great the heavens shook with the sound of thunder.

As the lightning bolts and thunder clashed, rain began to fall. Amid this distraction, Moni Mekhala collected her crystal ball from the sky and made her escape into the clouds.

It was not long before Ream Eyso regained his bearings. As he wiped the rain from his eyes, he realized his foe had escaped. He grabbed his axe and flew into the clouds, vowing to challenge the goddess another time.

From this day onward, when dark clouds form in the sky, lightning, thunder and rain are all that we mortals see of the eternal battle between the water goddess and the giant storm demon.

ACKNOWLEDGEMENTS

Troll by Theo

We want to thank all our Forest School kids for making our days out and about in the woods so magical, especially during 2020 where it brought some uplifting normality to an otherwise unprecedented, challenging year!

We want to thank our son Theo for not only helping us invent new games like Feed the Fire, but also for his love and ever-deepening knowledge and enthusiasm for the natural world. We also wanted to say a big thank you to our good friends and Forest School assistants: Nicole Ormerod for her joyful energy and Asa Marks for her kindness and insightful care.

PLAY THE FOREST SCHOOL WAY

This bestselling book will get kids outside, making and building in the real world. Offering ideas for groups of all sizes, the activities provide fantastic opportunities for family time and days out, whether your local woodland is a forest or a strip of trees. This was the first book to share Forest School games, crafts and skill-building activities with families and friends. Its magical illustrations and simple instructions will draw children into a world of wonder and encourage them to fall in love with outdoor play.

A YEAR OF FOREST SCHOOL

Rain or shine, this book will get kids playing outdoors, developing new skills and discovering the wonder of nature across the year! Written for parents, teachers and anyone else who wants to try out Forest School activities, and also as a handy resource for Forest School leaders, it follows on from *Play the Forest School Way*, with brand-new crafts, games and survival skills that connect with the natural cycle of the year. For each season, there's also a special day out which is a multi-activity session.

FOREST SCHOOL ACTIVITY CARDS

The first-ever Forest School-themed activity card deck. Pocket-sized, beautifully designed and packed with ideas.

Find out more about Jane Worroll and Peter Houghton's Forest School via email: theforestschoolway@gmail.com **website:** www.theforestschoolway.com
facebook.com/theforestschoolway instagram.com/theforestschoolway